GOOD MOTHER'S GUIDE TO RAISING A GOOD STUDENT

Vicki Poretta & Marian Edelman Borden

CASTLE BOOKS

Originally published as *Mom's Guide* ™ *to Raising A Good Student*

This edition published in 2002 by
CASTLE BOOKS
A division of Book Sales, Inc.
114 Northfield Avenue
Edison, New Jersey 08837

This edition published by arrangement with and permission of
Wiley Publishing, Inc.
909 Third Avenue
New York, New York 10022

ISBN: 0-7858-1545-7

Printed in the United States of America

Dear Mom:

If you're like most moms, you probably greet September with mixed emotions. Sure, it's great that your kids are back in school, but it's also time for homework hassles, math problems that seem insolvable to anyone over 30, and science projects that leave kitchens a mess and kids in tears.

We're here to help you cope. We've been there and done that with our own kids. We'd like to share our strategies to help your children become the good students they must be to compete in the real world. We'll teach you how to make sure the educational system meets your child's needs. We'll tell you what has worked—and what hasn't.

What is a good student? A child who is eager to learn, is self-motivated, assumes responsibility for assignments, and takes pride in his or her work. That child is a good student, no matter what grades appear on his or her report card.

You will be your child's first—and most important—teacher. Although your math may be shaky and you may blank out on historical dates, your child will learn from you the importance and value of education. You will establish the foundation for a lifelong love of learning.

We wish we could offer you a guarantee that if you follow our suggestions, your child will become a straight-A student and win a full scholarship to college. (If you find a book like that, please let us know—we could use it for our own kids!) But what you will find in the chapters ahead are strategies to help your children excel and feel good about themselves as learners.

Helping our kids succeed in school is one of our most important parenting jobs. We're glad to help. Good luck!

Vicki Poretta

Marian Edelman Borden

Contents

Introduction

Although your kids may be the ones who attend classes every day, their education most definitely involves you. Consider: the science projects that have required the patience of Job and the knowledge of Einstein (who else but you has those characteristics?), the hours spent supervising homework and drilling multiplication tables, and the dozens of class trips and PTA bake sales that you support.

Being serious about your child's studies take a commitment of time and energy, and carving out moments in your busy schedule to spend quality time with your kids is tough. But helping your children become good students pays off not only in better grades for your kids, but also in closer ties for the entire family. The suggestions in this book will help you use your student's schoolwork to enrich your relationship. As you work together on projects, discuss what's going on in school, and extend your child's classroom learning through family trips, you'll learn your child's strengths, weaknesses, interests, and abilities...as well as your own.

You'll also find that by helping your child learn, you learn too! Your child can become the teacher and introduce you to subjects that weren't even invented when you were in school.

There will be times when you can't tolerate the idea of helping with one more book report, or when the drudgery of supervising daily homework gets you down (think how your child feels!). But as your child discovers the joy of learning, you'll know that you have given your child the greatest gift of all. You have raised not only a good student, but also a productive, successful member of society.

EXTRAS

Scattered throughout the text of the *Mom's Guide to Raising a Good Student*, you'll find helpful sidebars with useful information, including side "chats" with suggestions on how to help your student and danger signs that may mean your student is headed for trouble. Look for these features:

MOM KNOWS BEST

Tips and suggestions that will help you raise a good student.

MOM ALWAYS SAID

Cautions that will warn you against making common parenting mistakes.

WISE WORDS

Definitions that every mom should know.

ALL IN THE FAMILY

Extra information or anecdotes that give you the inside scoop on raising a good student.

Acknowledgments

Vicki Poretta wishes to acknowledge her husband, Joe, and their two children for their inspiration in the creation of the *Mom's Guide* series. Vicki also wishes to acknowledge John Rourke, Joe Fallon, and Henry Poydar of Big World Media, Inc., for their creative development and marketing of related *Mom's Guide* publications and products. She would also like to thank her friends at Poretta and Orr, Inc., especially Peter Laughton, for their creative help. Vicki also wishes to thank her many "sports mom" friends who lent their support and ideas along the cheering sidelines of their kids' games.

This book wouldn't have been possible without the help and advice of many families who shared their secrets for raising good students. Marian Edelman Borden greatly appreciates their advice and good humor.

Most especially, Marian wants to thank her own "good students": Dan, Maggie, Sam, and Charles. They've taught her more than she ever learned in a classroom, and the education she's had since giving birth to each of them has been the most rewarding of her life. They are her inspiration and delight.

Of course, the above mentioned "good students" wouldn't be possible without John, their father and Marian's best friend. His editorial advice is without peer, and his support and encouragement made this book possible.

Thanks to Kate Kelly, who suggested Marian for this project. Kate, the mother of three "good students," is the author of *The Complete Idiot's Guide to Parenting a Teenager.*

The writing life can be a very solitary existence, but less so thanks to the members of the Westchester Writers Group, who listen and encourage Marian every month, and to Dan Carlinsky of the American Society of Journalists and Authors, who is always available for writers in crisis. Marian also wants to thank Diane Friedman, Judy Gartman, Myra Harris, and Carole Springer for their help with the chapter on learning disabilities.

Finally, to all the good, caring teachers who have graced the classrooms of Marian's children, know that you have made a difference—and thank you.

The Fine Art of Raising a Good Student

Some kids are blessed with brains. They bring home straight A's on their report cards without cracking a book. But that doesn't make them good students.

A good student is a child who is *self-motivated* to learn, *takes responsibility* for his assignments, and *takes pride* in his work.

Are good students born that way, or does it take mom-effort to produce them? Without question, what you do at home—the lessons *you* teach about responsibility, effort, and pride and the model of intellectual curiosity you set—makes all the difference when it comes to what kind of student your child will be.

1

LEARNING BEGINS AT HOME

Sometimes moms need to spell it out, point blank: *Education is important in our family. We expect you to do your best. We know you can.*

It's as simple as that in some ways, a lot more complicated in others. But making sure your kids know, in word and deed, that you take schoolwork seriously and expect them to do the same is the very first step to raising a good student. Here's how to send that message:

- ◆ *Ask about your child's schoolwork daily.* Not just about homework; inquire about the subjects she's studying.

- ◆ *Let your child see* you *learning.* Let her see you looking something up in the encyclopedia or checking a spelling in the dictionary.

- ◆ *Go back to school yourself,* even if it's to take a nonacademic subject that interests you.

- ◆ Talk about higher education with your child. Just watching a college football game on TV together can be an opportunity to talk about education.

MOM ALWAYS SAID

Sports and outside activities are important, but don't let them take priority over education. When push comes to shove, make sure school comes first.

FRIENDS MAKE THE GRADE

Your child's friends also influence his outlook on academic performance. Some kids will deliberately restrain their academic interest and achievement rather than be cut off from a popular crowd. Even the most popular kid worries that he will be considered a "nerd."

If your child's pals are academically motivated, then it's more likely that your child will be, too. Friendship is based on more than academic achievement, but encouraging your child to select friends who share her commitment to school is another way to send a positive message about education. Here's how to encourage these new friendships:

◆ *Suggest that your child hold a study group at your house to prepare for an upcoming test.* Snacks, also known as "brain food," should be kid-oriented (no carrot sticks!).

◆ *Enroll your student in an academically oriented after-school program.* The kids your child meets under these circumstances may have more in common with her scholastically than the usual crowd.

His Friends Couldn't Care Less!

Not all your child's friends will necessarily feel as motivated about school as he does, nor should they be. A well-rounded kid has friends who connect with many different aspects of his personality. But if you're worried that he's running with a crowd who couldn't care less about school, here are some things to keep in mind:

◆ *Be careful about criticizing your child's friends.* It can cause a problem between you and your child.

◆ *As much as possible, trust your child's judgment.* When you can back off a little and let him come to his own conclusion about a friend you don't particularly like, he may well agree with you.

◆ *Encourage him to make new friends.* This doesn't necessarily mean leaving the old ones behind.

◆ *Take the time to know your child's friends.* You may discover the attributes that your child finds interesting. For example, the friend who doesn't talk at all or dresses outrageously may be a computer whiz or an incredible athlete.

SHE'S GOTTA WANT TO LEARN

You can lead a horse to water but you can't make him drink, the old saying goes. No matter how much you want a child to learn, eventually that commitment to learning has to come from within.

Your child has to *want* to be a good student. Here's how you can encourage her to become self-motivated.

Ready, Set, Goal

Achievers set goals for themselves—so do good students. Before the school year begins, talk to your student about her academic goals for the year. The emphasis shouldn't be on grades. It can include not only what will be taught in the classroom, but also what your student plans to study on her own. Write the list down and post it where your student can monitor her own progress.

For example, "By the end of the school year, I plan to":

◆ Read all the books by Roald Dahl.

◆ Learn long division.

◆ Practice my piano 20 minutes a day.

◆ Kick (at least) one soccer goal this season.

MOM KNOWS BEST

Encourage your student to read biographies of people he admires. Biographies can be fun—and inspiring, too. Start young; there are books out there for all ages.

Focus on the Attainable

It's important that kids (and adults) have dreams. If your child declares at the age of four that she wants to be a doctor, good for her! But you also want your student to set manageable, short-term goals. For one thing, success is self-reinforcing. When your child sets goals and then achieves them, she'll carry the positive lesson all her life. Concept will become reality for her, while repeated practice will teach her the steps necessary to make her dreams come true.

Here's something you can try with your student to give him some practice in establishing his priorities and organizing his time. On Sunday, set a goal for that week and write it down. Talk about what needs to be done. For example, if he has a book report due on Friday, do the following:

♦ *Discuss how he plans to accomplish the goal.*

♦ *Break the goal down into smaller steps.* Will he finish reading the book by Tuesday? Write the first draft on Wednesday? Revise and print out the final copy on Thursday?

♦ *Talk about how he's doing as the week progresses* and what problems, if any, he's encountering in his quest for the goal. Does he need to cut back on TV in order to reach his goal?

♦ *Review what happened at the end of the week,* and evaluate how he did. Praise him for trying. Set a new goal for the next week.

Success—It Adds Up

Sometimes kids will get discouraged when they fail to accomplish one of their goals. It's up to you to remind them how far they've come. If your student is struggling with a difficult book, remind him of when he couldn't even read! Or when he had just begun to read books without illustrations! Kids need to measure success in comparative terms, not just in absolutes.

It's easy to get dazzled by good grades. But if we only recognize high achievement, then we limit rewards to a select few. Not every effort your student makes will necessarily result in an A or B, and that's not the point anyway.

You and your child want to recognize progress. If her goal is spelling every word on her spelling test correctly, then chart her improvement and celebrate her progress when she succeeds in getting 8 out of 10, up from 6 out of 10 the week before.

CHEERING HER ON

It doesn't take Einstein to prove this theory:

> **The key to success, academic or otherwise,
> is believing in yourself.**

And here's the corollary: Kids who believe in themselves have moms who believe in them!

From the first time a mom cheers at her baby's smile (what an accomplishment!), a child learns that he's special. Kids need to know that their mom's love is absolutely unconditional, that they're valued for just being themselves, not for their grades, not for their accomplishments. When a child knows that her parents care and think she's special, she believes it, too. It's liberating.

Offering unconditional love does *not* mean you condone misbehavior. Kids live up to expectations—good or bad. Tell your child when his behavior or attitude is inappropriate, but always make clear that you're criticizing the behavior, not the child.

MOM ALWAYS SAID

To emphasize that each of their children is special, parents sometimes assign each one a specific role, like athlete, or student. Don't pigeonhole this way. It puts limits on kids.

Believe in Your Kids

It's really important that you assure your kids by your words and your actions that you believe they're capable of accomplishing their goals. When they doubt their own abilities, you're going to be their bedrock of confidence. If you don't believe in them, who will? Use words like, "I know you can," when your child sets a goal for herself. Increase her freedom—and her responsibility—as her maturity increases. Your student will get the message that you have faith in her ability to make good decisions.

Who's in Charge Here?

Kids need to know that the grown-ups are in charge and that there are rules in the family. Children find it scary when no limits exist. Just establishing rules about homework, TV, and family meals teaches a child that his parents are concerned about him—that he's special. Limits give kids the freedom to focus on learning.

On the other hand, kids also need to see that their mom is flexible enough to bend or change the limits when necessary.

ALL IN THE FAMILY

Here are six sentences that build self-esteem:

♦ You can do it if you try.

♦ Knowing you, it will be fine.

♦ You'll figure it out.

♦ I can see that you tried really hard.

♦ You can learn something valuable from every mistake.

♦ I'm proud of you for trying hard.

Writing Your Child's Story

A great parent-child project is a scrapbook of your student's interests and accomplishments. Again, it's more than pasting in good report cards. Encourage your youngster to keep a record of the books she has read, the places she has traveled, and her favorite drawings. This gives your student her own record of success and helps her chart her progress.

Writing her own autobiography—and updating it each year—is a great way for your child to see herself as important and valuable. When she's younger, she can dictate the story to you and illustrate it. As she matures, she can write it herself.

GET REAL, MOM

Moms can cheer for their kids in their sleep. "Good job!" "Way to go!" "Fabulous!" Sometimes praise can be almost too reflexive. Of course we want our children to feel good about themselves. Empty praise, though, isn't the way to go about it. Kids know the difference when they hear compliments that are deserved and those that aren't. When they hear praise offered for modest or even no achievement, all praise starts to become meaningless. They may come to the conclusion that they have no ability and their mom is just trying to make them feel better.

Other children become addicted to praise, constantly seeking it for every effort ("Was I the best?"). Some will deliberately criticize themselves ("I'm the worst speller in my class.") so their mom will correct them with praise ("No, honey, you're really a spelling champ.").

Kids addicted to praise are less likely to take risks that would help them learn and grow. They may read an easier book or take a less challenging course in order to receive praise.

Real Praise

When you do praise your children, keep these tips in mind:

♦ *Be specific in your praise.* Instead of saying, "What a fabulous picture," say, "I like the way you used red in the painting," or, "That design is really unusual."

♦ *Describe what it is you like, rather than the product.* Instead of saying, "You wrote a great report," you might say, "I can see you really put a lot of research into your report on kangaroos. I didn't know a baby kangaroo is called a joey." This tells your student that you admire her research skills and shows that you were really paying attention.

♦ *Don't give praise in comparison to another child.* When you tell your student, "You're a better writer than your friend Jill," you foster an unnecessary competition. It may also make her worry about failure if she meets a more talented writer.

♦ *Don't dilute your praise by pointing out problems in the same breath.* Giving "left-handed" compliments, pointing out, "You're terrific at math, but you really need to work on your writing skills," is disappointing and frustrating. Let your student enjoy a moment of glory.

Failure Isn't a Dirty Word

Kids need to learn that making a mistake isn't the end of the world. As Thomas J. Watson, the founder of IBM, once said, "Would you like me to give you a formula for success? It's quite simple, really. Double your rate of failure." To be a successful student—or adult— you have to be willing to take risks. Living up to your potential means facing potential failures and learning from them. The author is unknown, but the truth is "Most successes are built on a multitude of failures."

ENCOURAGING THE RESPONSIBLE CHILD

You want your student to be responsible for his schoolwork. One way to help him learn responsibility is to assign household chores to every member of the family. For example, by third grade a child can set and clear the table, take out the garbage, and keep his room neat. As he gets older, his household responsibilities can increase.

Besides providing much-needed help with the chores, what does assigning chores accomplish? It sends the message, *I trust you.* Your child learns that you believe in his ability to get things done. This applies to his room and his homework.

Remember, Mom: Nagging is a no-no. If you're constantly checking to make sure the task is done or redoing it *your way*, then the lesson of responsible behavior is lost. Post a chart on the refrigerator listing the week's chores and the person assigned to each job. If the task isn't completed, be clear in advance what the consequences will be and follow through with them.

MOM KNOWS BEST

When assigning chores, make sure yours is an equal-opportunity household. Boys need to know how to cook, girls need to know how to mow the lawn, and the same educational standards apply to all.

Beyond the Bare Minimum

You want your child to try her best with whatever job she undertakes. That doesn't mean perfection. Let your child know that you expect her to do a job that she's proud to call her own.

Some kids always do their homework but do the very least that's required. If the teacher requires at least five words in a sentence for spelling homework, five words is all you ever see. That's frustrating, especially when you know your child is capable of more.

Encourage your student to do more, and reward him with honest praise when he does. Don't expect big leaps in accepting additional homework responsibility, but look for steady progress. If he writes one sentence with eight words instead of the required five, that's cause for acknowledgment.

Some kids are willing to do the work but don't care how the finished product looks. Let your child know that a composition full of cross-outs detracts from his message. Pride in appearance—both his own and his work—is important.

Do It Again—Better

It can cause a major battle, but sometimes you have to insist that your student try again or do the assignment over. Just because the work meets the teacher's standards doesn't necessarily mean it meets yours.

It's a balancing act, of course. (Most of parenting is.) You don't want to be a demanding taskmaster, but you do want your student to stretch and do his best. Pay attention to what you say and how he responds. Learn when to push and when to stop.

You know your child. You know if your child needs a gentle prodding in order to encourage her to do her best. (You may also know if your child is the type who could use a little more than a gentle prod!) "Pushy moms" get a bad rap, but sometimes kids need someone to tell them to do it again...and again.

Be alert for signs of stress if you think your child is under too much pressure (from the school or you). Some common indications of stress are:

◆ Cries easily

◆ Needs constant reassurance and praise

◆ Develops a nervous tic

◆ Tells lies

◆ Withdraws

◆ Acts belligerent

If your child exhibits any of these symptoms, try to find out what's bothering him. You may need to consult your pediatrician and the teacher and develop a plan to relieve some of the pressure.

THE BOOB TUBE

TV gets a bad rap from most moms. It's a distraction from serious studying, a mindless escape. Is the answer no TV? Should the TV dial be programmed for educational channels only? Get real.

TV, in moderation, can be a learning experience:

◆ For the young viewer, TV can be a source of language.

◆ TV can expose kids to other cultures and positive social values; it can be a source of information about the world.

◆ TV can be a resource for learning about nature, history, current events, music, drama, and art.

◆ If viewed as a family, TV can act as a springboard for discussions about values. *Talk about what you and your child are seeing—even the commercials.* One mom discovered that when she watched *Beverly Hills 90210* with her preteen son, they had substantive conversations about sex, drugs, and academics. "We discussed lots of topics that would have normally been a big turn-off if I had brought up the subjects, but that were perfectly reasonable to discuss in the context of Brandon and Kelly!"

MOM KNOWS BEST

Some research suggests that children who watch a moderate amount of TV actually perform better in school than non-viewers. TV provides more sources of information. Predictably, those children who are glued to the set suffer academically, says the American Psychological Association's Task Force on Television and Society.

Tuned In—But with Family

One of the best ways to keep TV viewing under control is to keep the set out of your child's room. When the TV is in a student's room, viewing becomes unlimited and unsupervised. Furthermore, a child is more likely to become isolated, closeted with his TV, rather than with family.

Setting the Rules

To help your student keep TV in perspective, establish family rules about TV viewing:

- ◆ Insist that homework is done before the TV goes on.

- ◆ Set limits on how much TV is permissible. A general rule of thumb is no more than two hours on a school night.

- ◆ Don't permit TV to interfere with family time. Dinner means the TV is off. If a favorite show or educational offering is on at an inconvenient time, offer to tape the show. This shows your child you respect his interests, while keeping TV in perspective for your family.

MOM ALWAYS SAID

By the time your child graduates from high school he will have watched between 15,000 to 18,000 hours of TV, compared with 11,000 hours of classroom instruction.

THE LEAST YOU NEED TO KNOW

- ◆ A good student is self-motivated and responsible and takes pride in his work.

- ◆ Education is a family priority. Schoolwork takes precedence over outside activities and sports.

- ◆ Build your child's self-esteem by offering real praise for real accomplishments. Avoid meaningless cheerleading.

- ◆ Celebrate effort and trying hard, not just good grades.

- ◆ TV can be a learning tool when parents monitor content and watch with their kids.

2

Time to Get Organized!

Your child's first teacher is *you*, and her first school is at home. Creating a comfortable home study center, stocked with supplies and reference materials, makes it easier for your child to do her homework and pursue independent learning. Even more important, by creating this environment you send a clear message to your student: learning begins at home.

CLEAR THE TABLE, IT'S HOMEWORK TIME

Where your child does homework is a function of space and inclination—yours and his. Some families prefer their kids to work at the kitchen table in full view of mom, who can answer any questions and keep the student on task. This is probably most important in the early grades. As your child gets older, your goal is to have him work independently, perhaps in his own room or in another area of the house designated for homework.

Wherever a child does his homework, that place should be free of distractions—at least for the time that the work is being done. If he's working in a central location in the house, such as the living room, the TV should be off and general family chit-chat should be moved to another room. If you choose to use this time to do your own paperwork or to read, you can keep him company and serve as a great role model at the same time.

MOM KNOWS BEST

Some straight-A students study sprawled on the floor with music blaring. If that's how your child learns best, don't argue—even if it seems against the laws of nature! Find what works and go with it.

What's Needed?

Even if your child does his homework at the kitchen table, provide him with a desk and chair, if possible. Apart from being a good place for papers, school supplies, and reference books, a desk makes a statement about your family's commitment to education.

Here are the furniture basics of a good study center:

◆ Desk

◆ Comfortable chair

◆ Storage space for supplies and papers

◆ Bookshelves

◆ Desk lamp

◆ Bulletin board

◆ Computer station (optional)

The Desk Set

When desk shopping, you don't have to go for anything elaborate. Look for something, new or used, that's solid, clean, and splinter-free. Or you could make your own desk. Buy a flat, sturdy door—

that's right, I said "door"—and lay it across two two-drawer file cabinets. Presto! A large, flat surface for art projects and plenty of room to spread out when working on a report. You can get a door at any big hardware store. Be sure and buy one that doesn't have raised molding.

The chair should be comfortable and fit easily under the desk. Have your child test it out before you buy it to make sure it provides good lower back support. If you plan to have a computer station in the same area, it's best to go for a swivel chair on wheels so the child moves easily between the two work areas. The chair should be adjustable so that your child can vary the height as she grows. When she's seated with her feet on the floor, her thighs should be parallel to the floor. Fewer back problems later.

Tiny Budget?

Don't freak out, Mom, there's no need to invest your whole fortune in a desk and chair. The Salvation Army, newspaper want ads, garage sales, community bulletin boards, and the dumpster outside an apartment building—these are all good sources for furniture. Large corporations also often sell their office furniture when they downsize or move.

ALL IN THE FAMILY

One mom discovered fabulous furniture finds when she began driving through her neighborhood the night before bulk-trash pickup day. She lugged home a great wooden desk in her station wagon and sponge-painted it to match her daughter's room decor. It looked great!

A Useful Place to Put Things In

Drawers are key. A simple filing system, one you and your student develop together (such as file folders labeled for spelling, current events, science projects, etc.), will help your child keep her papers organized. If the desk area doesn't have any storage space, buy a file box; a stationery or office supply store will have ones for under $20.

At the end of the year, save papers and mementos of the school year in accordion file folders with elastic wraps. Label the folders with your child's name and the year and store them out of the way. Who knows, you may want them again.

Books and Shelves

A sturdy bookcase can be a family heirloom or an artistic arrangement of bricks and boards. Here are some installation tips:

◆ *Make the shelves easily accessible.* Avoid building shelves over a desk if it means your elementary-age child has to climb on a chair to reach a book.

◆ *Centralize the reference materials in the living room or family study area* so the entire family can use them.

◆ *Provide at least a couple of shelves in each child's room* for her personal reading material.

◆ *Establish a house rule about where library books are kept.* Countless fines later, one family put a cardboard box in the hallway for all library books. The house rule was that library books were to be kept in the box, taken out for each reading, and then returned. No more lost or late books!

Shedding Light on the Subject

A good desk lamp eases eye strain. Even if you have overhead lighting, you'll still want a good desk lamp. An incandescent light bulb gives softer light than a fluorescent one. Put the lamp on the left side of the desk for right-handed kids, on the right for lefties, to get rid of annoying shadows as your child writes.

Tack It Up

If you have room, include a bulletin board in your study center. Be sure to post a calendar so your student can mark test dates, long-term project schedules, notices, good papers, and, of course, school vacations!

THE WELL-APPOINTED STUDENT

Establishing an organized, well-equipped study center at home makes homework much easier, but you also want to make sure your student has the materials she needs to work effectively at school. Check out office supply "supermarkets" for good prices on basic supplies; local stores may also run specials on school supplies during the last weeks of summer. You may have to wait until school starts to purchase certain items, since some teachers like to make specific suggestions about supplies on the first day of class.

Stock up on markers, crayons, pencils, loose-leaf paper, construction paper, glue sticks, a ruler, a stapler, scissors, file folders, binders, poster board, etc. At the beginning of the school year you can often find these things at a discount. Stockpile old magazines, if you have any; they can come in handy for projects. Homework and assignments are much easier to complete when materials are easily accessible.

When the Price Is Right, Stock Up

Generations of families have marked the end of summer and the start of the new school year with a day of shopping for new clothes and supplies. It's a great way to help your kids make the transition. Items to shop for may include:

- A backpack (big enough to hold a lunch box and snack for younger kids and loads of books for older students)
- Book covers (unless you want to use plain brown bags to cover textbooks)
- Spiral notebooks for each subject or a loose-leaf binder with subject dividers
- Pens, pencils, markers, and crayons
- Erasers
- A pencil sharpener (You may want to invest in an electric one for home use, but your student will still need a small, portable one for school.)
- A ruler
- A pencil holder
- A protractor and calculator (for older students)

Keeping Track

In the younger grades, students may write their daily assignments in the same book in which they do their homework. But for older students, a small (3" × 5") assignment book to record daily and long-term homework is helpful. Suggest your student write down the date on which the assignment is given, what the assignment is, the due date, and when he handed the assignment in. Be a good model, Mom! Keep a to-do list on the fridge and check items off every day.

With students in the younger grades, ask to check their homework assignments daily so you can see what needs to be done and encourage planning for long-term projects. With an older student you'll want to check the organizer early in the school year to make sure he's marking down what needs to be done, but the goal is to have him assume responsibility for his assignments.

Now That You're Organized...

Having set up an organized home study center and bought the supplies your student will need, the next step is to figure out how to maintain the system for more than one day.

◆ *Ask that your student keep her desk clutter-free.* Using it as a convenient dumping place for laundry sort of defeats its purpose.

◆ *Establish a system about where your child will put her backpack, lunch box, and school notices* when she first comes home from school.

◆ *Cut down on "morning crazies"* by having your child pack everything up the night before and put what is needed for school by the door.

MOM'S LIBRARY CHECKLIST

Invest in certain basic reference materials for your home. Having ready access to these books will cut down on stress, especially on Sunday nights when the library is closed and the big project is due Monday morning. Having reference materials around the house—especially if your student sees *you* using them—sends a strong pro-learning message.

ALL IN THE FAMILY

One mom's holiday tradition helped build her family's home library. Each year she bought them all a hardcover edition of a classic book—*Charlotte's Web* and *The Phantom Tollbooth* when her kids were young, *Treasure Island, Huck Finn,* and *Catcher in the Rye* as they grew older.

Look It Up

When your student is in elementary school, you'll want to have two dictionaries in the house: a *children's dictionary,* with simple definitions, large print, and pictures, and an *adult dictionary,* because kids often ask about words that are more sophisticated than will be found in a kid's version. Invest in hardcover copies of each. They should be well-worn by the time your child finishes high school.

Even young students can benefit from a good *thesaurus.* It enriches written reports and expands a youngster's vocabulary.

An *atlas* is essential; if you have a good place to put one, a *large world map* is also very handy. Among other purposes, it can be used to track family travels or global expeditions. One mom laminated a paper map of the world and used it to cover the kitchen table. It gave a decidedly "foreign" atmosphere to family dinners.

An *encyclopedia* is a great resource, especially for younger students. For kids in the upper grades working on research projects, encyclopedia entries offer a condensed overview of their topic and a list of suggested readings, which is a great way to get started on a new subject.

Ask at the bookstore for recommendations. There are one or two excellent one-volume encyclopedias on the market. Or you might watch for used book sales at your local library or college. Even if an encyclopedia is 10 years old, most of the material in it will still be valid. One family bought a 7-year-old encyclopedia set for $10. Brand new, the set would have cost close to $1,000!

Building a Home Library

Other books that can help your child in her studies:

◆ A book of quotations

◆ A style handbook for term papers

◆ The Bible (many literary references are biblically based)

◆ The complete works of Shakespeare

◆ An almanac

◆ A foreign language dictionary when your children start studying another language

◆ A guide to whichever word processing program you use

TO COMPUTER OR NOT TO COMPUTER?

Computer literacy has become as important as learning to read and write. All high school graduates are expected to be able to use a computer, at least for basic word processing. The question is, does your third grader need one? If at all possible, yes.

Computers can be a lot of fun, but more than that, they're a powerful learning tool. For example:

◆ Reading, math, and geometry games teach skills and get information across in an entertaining way. For older students, there are SAT tutoring programs and other useful products on the market.

◆ Reference materials on CD-ROM, such as Encarta or Compton's, offer effective and up-to-date sources of information.

◆ A computer allows your student to focus on the creative side of writing assignments without the drudgery and arguments over handwriting. And it makes revisions so much easier! Even younger students are often willing to spend time revising and refining their written work when they can do so using the simple cut and paste operations of a word processor.

◆ Online resources like America Online's "homework help" can be a lifesaver when it's nine o'clock at night and Mom doesn't understand sixth-grade math.

◆ Using a computer can train your student to be a faster typist, especially if he's allowed to "chat" online. Keeping up with the conversation takes nimble fingers!

At a minimum, you want a machine your child can use to write reports and eventually term papers. Most teachers in the upper grades expect papers to be typed. With limited funds you can purchase a word processor (some retail for less than $200) or a used computer from someone who's upgrading.

MOM KNOWS BEST

Should you get a Macintosh or a PC computer? Macs are easier to learn and use, but most offices use PCs. Your call.

Buying a New Computer

If you're going to buy a new computer, one which your student can use to surf the Internet, play games, create charts, word process, etc., then you'll need a machine with a minimum of:

◆ 16 megabytes of RAM

◆ A 1.2 gigabyte hard drive

◆ A Pentium or similar chip

◆ A 33.6 kbps modem

◆ An 8X-CD-ROM

You may want to add a 16-bit Sound Blaster Card with speakers to turn your computer into a multimedia center.

And here's one other factor to consider: obsolescence. Discouraging but true: Technology is advancing so fast these days that the consumer may find her nice new computer out of date before she can even get it out to the car. Your best bet is to get one that can be upgraded easily. It may be more expensive in the short term, but at least you won't find yourself replacing the entire system a year or two later. To avoid getting stuck with a dinosaur, ask the salesperson:

- How easy it is to upgrade the computer
- Whether it has expansion slots for extra devices
- Whether it will accept generic parts

Setting Up

To avoid repetitive stress injuries and prevent back and neck strain, you want to be sure that your computer is set up for maximum comfort. Here's how:

- If you're setting up your home computer next to your student's desk, put the computer table to the left of the desk (if she's right-handed).
- The keyboard should be at elbow level so that the user's hands rest comfortably on it. Add a keyboard extender (which attaches under the computer table and pulls out) if the computer table is too high.
- The user's eyes should focus down slightly on the computer screen. To make sure the computer screen is at the right height, place the top of the screen at eye level or slightly down.

Hers or Ours?

Do you want the computer to be accessible to everyone in the family, or just your student? If there's only one computer in the house, you'll probably choose the former. Having the computer in a central location also allows you to monitor its use and keeps your student from spending hours alone with the computer, away from the rest of the family.

Still, in some households, putting a computer in the student's room works just fine. It's up to you, Mom. But wherever you put the computer, do be sure and establish house rules for its use.

MOM ALWAYS SAID

Don't put the computer on your student's desk, unless it's one of those L-shaped desks where the computer is off to one side. Otherwise there'll be no room left to spread out.

Surfing the Net

Elementary students across the nation were part of a South Pole expedition, keeping daily logs and chatting with the explorers via the Net; others students have "talked" to astronauts while in space; still others have had online interviews with popular authors.

The resources of the Internet are vast, but there's also potential for abuse. There are places you don't want your student to "go" on the Internet and strangers you don't want her (or him) to "talk" to. Some Net surfers have the worst of intentions. Be clear which sites and chat rooms your student can visit. (Most services permit parents to limit access to cyberporn sites.) Here are some other ground rules you can lay down in advance or even post near the computer:

◆ Never give out your full name, address, or home telephone number to anyone you meet online.

◆ Never give out your user password to anyone.

◆ If you meet someone online who tries to steer the conversation into a sexual pick-up, *turn off the computer and report the incident to your parents.*

ALL IN THE FAMILY

Young girls and boys show equal interest in computers, but by early adolescence the computer rooms at school tend to end up with an imbalance of boys. Moms can help beat the trend by encouraging their daughters to use the computer at home and after school.

Sticker Shock?

Okay, so you can't afford a computer. It's not a crisis. Many public schools have computers that students can use after school and during the lunch hour. Public libraries are a good resource, and you can also rent computer time at some copy centers. Hey, want to do something really cool? Check out the new cybercafes! The kid logs on while you have a cup of coffee...and maybe snatch a peek at the Net yourself.

THE LEAST YOU NEED TO KNOW

- ◆ Helping your student become organized pays off in time saved later for studying.

- ◆ A home study center should be comfortable and well stocked with books and supplies.

- ◆ Some students study best at a desk in a quiet room; others need music in the background and a floor to sprawl on. Figure out what works best for your student.

- ◆ Computers have become essential study tools. Fortunately, lots of options exist for getting access to one.

3

Hassle-Free Homework

Homework, as any kid knows, interferes with TV watching, video game playing, and "serious hanging out." Homework, as any mom knows, frequently reduces her to the role of prison warden, guarding the "inmate" who is assigned to the academic equivalent of a chain gang.

Homework should reinforce and advance what's being taught in the classroom. Sometimes the assignments are boring and require rote memorization—the multiplication tables, for instance. Sometimes they're interesting and even inspiring. Either way, they have to get done.

WHAT'S THE POINT?

Homework has many purposes. It's an opportunity to:

◆ Practice skills not yet completely learned.

◆ Review skills the student might forget.

◆ Enrich and broaden knowledge of a subject.

◆ Teach responsibility and organizational skills.

◆ Complete classwork.

Homework should never be a time to master material that has not been presented in class.

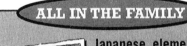

ALL IN THE FAMILY

Japanese elementary students spend at least twice as much time on homework as American students do.

GET THE SKINNY ON HOMEWORK *EARLY*

If your child's school doesn't hold a Back-to-School Night, call and ask the teacher for her homework policy. You want to know:

◆ How much homework she assigns each night.

◆ How much time she expects students to spend on homework nightly.

◆ How much parental involvement she wants. Some teachers prefer that parents not correct homework; others welcome the parental input—within reason, of course.

HOW MUCH HOMEWORK?

Many school systems establish homework guidelines for each grade. Of course, as one mom pointed out, her daughter could take five minutes of spelling homework and drag it out for four hours! Here are some guidelines:

- Grade 3: 30 minutes

- Grades 4 and 5: 45 to 60 minutes

- Grades 6, 7, and 8: 1 to 2 hours

- Grades 9, 10, 11, and 12: 2 to 3 hours

Another rule of thumb is to multiply your child's grade level by 10. That would mean a third grader should complete her homework in about 30 minutes, an eighth grader in an hour and 20 minutes.

Be realistic. Kids need time to relax after a hard day at school, so it's best to build in some "down time" before homework begins. Set up a schedule—a snack and a short bike ride, followed by homework, dinner, and TV would be one possibility—and then stick to it.

MOM KNOWS BEST

Thirty minutes of reading every day should be a permanent homework assignment. If the teacher doesn't assign it, you should.

PROCRASTINATION—DOESN'T EVERYONE?

It's hard not to sympathize with your student when she'd rather watch cartoons than memorize state capitals. Who wouldn't? But learning to prioritize is one of the most important lessons of homework assignments.

Before the school year begins, sit down with your student and decide *together* when homework will be done. You're more likely to get cooperation if you take into account the child's own preferences.

Like adults, kids procrastinate because:

- *They don't know how to do something.* Encourage your student to admit when she doesn't understand an assignment or the subject material and get help before the problem gets out of hand.

- *They would rather be doing something else (who wouldn't?).* Set clear rules about doing homework and stick to your guns. Make it clear that homework is a priority, even if it's boring.

- *They feel it has to be perfect—and it will take forever to be perfect, so why bother to try?* This kind of self-imposed pressure will carry over to other parts of her life, too. Talk with your student about the positive side of making mistakes. Encourage her to take pride in her work, but not to hold herself up to an impossible standard.

MOM ALWAYS SAID

A good student must be on time for school and prepared with homework assignments. If your child tends to procrastinate or dawdle, here's a game that teaches the value of planning ahead and being on time.

Have your child estimate how long she thinks it will take to carry out a few simple tasks—getting dressed in the morning, making a school lunch, driving to the grocery store, etc. Then use a clock to time each of these tasks. (It's more fun if you write down her estimates, too.) Remember, it's not a race; the point is to make the best guess ahead of time.

Sometimes you can help a procrastinator by brainstorming with her about tasks that can be done ahead of time, like putting out clothes the night before or assembling the ingredients for the lunch ahead of time. How about making a week's worth of lunches at a time?

Can't Sit Still

If your child has difficulty sitting still for an extended period of time, schedule breaks during homework time. If necessary, set a timer for 15 minutes and insist that your child work until the bell rings. After a 5-minute break, reset the timer for another 15 minutes.

Or break down the homework into subject areas so that she finishes her math before the break, then tackles her geography assignments. Always organize the homework by the most difficult tasks first—when your child is rested and least frustrated.

SINK OR SWIM

It's hard to watch your child struggle with an assignment, but before you jump in with help, WAIT. Part of any homework assignment is to learn *how* to approach a problem. You're there to lend a hand if the student is in over her head, but don't rush to the rescue. Often, with a little patience, your student can figure the problem out by herself. When you are too quick to jump in with help, your student may get the message, "I don't think you can do it."

Here are four steps to help your student help herself:

1. *Encourage her to explain the assignment.* For example, her homework might be to complete 10 math problems involving adding fractions.

2. *Break the process down into smaller parts.* Taking it step by step will help both of you focus on exactly what she doesn't understand. She may be clear that the denominators must be identical in order to complete the addition, but unclear about how to change the denominators.

3. *Explain the specific part of the sequence that your student doesn't understand.* Wait before going on to the next step to make sure she grasps what you've just reviewed and to see whether she can take the next step on her own.

4. *Have your student restate the explanation in her own words,* showing you how to complete another problem.

"Give someone a fish and you feed him for a day; teach him to fish and you'll feed him for a lifetime." Teaching your student to look words up herself gives her a lot more than she gets if you spell the word for her. This is her time to develop basic research and critical thinking skills. Give help as needed, while allowing her to develop these strengths.

When you review your child's homework, try to keep your suggestions general. For example, after reading a paragraph your student has written, you might say, "There are two periods missing. Can you find them?" This permits your child to take responsibility for reviewing his work and correcting his own errors.

"Are You Done with My Homework Yet, Mom?"

You need to communicate with your child's teacher if you find that your student is taking much longer to do her homework than the guidelines given at the beginning of the school year, or if he needs significant help to complete daily homework assignments.

Find out whether he's having difficulty keeping up with the class. If he's not having trouble academically and isn't dawdling over his assignments, it's possible that the teacher is assigning more homework than is reasonable. Talk to other parents in the class and see whether classmates are having similar problems. If so, you may need to alert the teacher.

On the other hand, this may simply be a temporary problem with this particular subject material. In any event, you will want to talk to the teacher about what steps you should take at home to help your student with homework.

ALL IN THE FAMILY

Here are some common reasons for homework trouble:

♦ Your child isn't paying attention in class.

♦ She has a learning problem.

♦ She's using homework difficulties to get *your* attention.

♦ The teacher is assigning homework material not yet taught.

♦ The assignment is unfair, unclear, or purposeless.

When Homework Becomes a Battleground

Sometimes a homework assignment or book report becomes too much of an issue and you need to back off. If you find that every correction or suggestion is met with an argument from your child, you may need to limit your involvement, at least for the time being. Sometimes an older sibling, a teen neighbor, or a grand-parent can step in and help with homework or short-term tutoring on a specific subject to relieve the tensions.

Sometimes a child's ego is so tied up in his work that he takes it personally when you offer advice. It may be wiser to let the teacher suggest changes, rather than have the homework assignment become a battleground. Again, keep the teacher informed.

MOM ALWAYS SAID

Encourage your student to complete the homework assignments of the subjects he likes *least*, first. He'll be less tired and less easily frustrated.

When Mom's Not Available

If you can't be around when your child does her homework, you can still supervise and help, even at a distance. Have your student call you when she comes home to talk about what happened at school and what homework has been assigned. Does she understand the material and the instructions? What is she going to do first? If necessary, help her prioritize her tasks. When you come home, ask to review her homework.

ALL IN THE FAMILY

One mother, on a business trip, had her son fax the first draft of a term paper to her hotel. Mom reviewed the assignment, made some suggestions, and then faxed it back home. E-mail works, too.

"WHERE DO I START?"

There are two basic rules for prioritizing homework. First, do the most difficult homework assignment first. Save the easier material for later and the extra credit for last.

Second, the day before a test, study exam material first. After completing the rest of the homework assignments, review the test material again or first thing the next morning.

MOM ALWAYS SAID

If your child is running into trouble with schoolwork, make sure the problem isn't with his hearing or vision, and don't rule out a learning disability. If there is a problem, you'll want to take prompt action.

HELP! MOM IS FLUNKING SIXTH-GRADE MATH

How can you help your child when you don't understand the material yourself? As your child progresses through the grades, you may feel less and less confident about your ability to answer questions. A new approach to math may leave you at a total loss: "That's not how *I* was taught to solve that problem!" Besides, sixth grade *was* kind of a long time ago...

Remember, if your child is having difficulty with a particular homework assignment, it may simply be a question of jogging his memory about the process. For example, if the student is having trouble with long division, and you have always suffered from a math phobia and have no clue about how to explain long division, ask him to "teach" you the process just as it was explained in class. The "teacher" will learn as much as the "student"!

Internet Solutions

For those with a computer and a modem, the Internet offers an array of tools for students. *Online homework help* is offered by online service providers like America Online, Prodigy, and CompuServe in the form of interactive resource rooms. If you log on and type in your question, experts in elementary, middle school, or high school will respond, usually the same day, with an answer or a suggestion about where to look for the answer.

America Online also offers resources like Barron's Notes (which offers helpful commentary on many of the novels read by students), as well as an encyclopedia, atlas, almanac, and other basic reference tools. Students can download and print out this information at any time, which is a blessing when it's 10 o'clock and your student suddenly remembers an assignment!

Cool Web Sites

Following are a few of the more useful Web sites out there. The Internet address is in boldface.

All-in-One Search Page: **http://www.albany.net/allinone**

This site compiles more than 120 search engines, databases, and indexes. Search categories you can click on include Software, Desk Reference, and Publications/Literature.

Yahoo!-Reference/Libraries: **http://www.yahoo.com/ Reference/Libraries**

Links to a large variety of libraries, including specialty holdings on medicine, science, law, and more.

Excite City.Net: **http://city.net/?**

Detailed geographical information on any place in the world.

TAMING TERM PAPER TRAUMAS

Lots of moms get nervous when their students bring home a term paper or research assignment that's to be done over several weeks. They can see it coming: the procrastination, the arguments, the "I can't DO this" attitude. The potential for homework hassles definitely increases with the complexity of the project.

What's the point, you may find yourself wondering as you drag your child to the library by her hair, of assigning third graders a report on their favorite animal? Actually, long-term projects teach a number of valuable skills, like how to budget time, break up a big project into manageable tasks, do basic research, take notes, write, and edit. These skills will prove invaluable as your student moves through high school and beyond.

Organize, Organize, Organize

To prevent the Big Project from turning into a Big Headache for you and your child, get organized. Help him break the assignment into parts. When the report is first assigned, take out a calendar, sit down with your student, and set deadlines for:

- Deciding on a topic
- Getting teacher approval
- Researching in the library and online
- Making contacts by mail or e-mail, as called for
- Taking notes
- Developing an outline
- Writing a first draft
- Making revisions
- Preparing the final copy
- Final proofreading

The teacher may assign a class schedule for each of these stages of a research project. If so, encourage your student to set his own deadlines at least a day earlier so he has time to review his work.

Make sure your student clearly understands the requirements for the project. He might want to make a list. Does it need:

- A title page?
- A table of contents?
- A bibliography?
- Illustrations?
- Footnotes?
- To be typed?

Whose Project Is It?

Every mom has seen science projects that scream *Parental Help!* It's hard not to get caught up in the desire to pitch in and make the project really outstanding. But moms also know that it doesn't really help any child.

It's okay to encourage your student to dig a little deeper, to try a little harder; just don't forget who the primary researcher is. Point out obvious grammatical or spelling errors, but be sure the language of the report reflects the student's age and sophistication, not yours. The illustrations, even if your child is not particularly artistic, should be her own.

If you have difficulty limiting your role in your student's long-term projects, the two of you may want to write and sign a contract outlining your responsibilities. When tensions arise about who, what, and when something needs to be done, you can simply refer to the contract.

Sample Contract

Project:_____

Date Assigned:_____

Date Due:_____

I _____ (*student's name*) will do the following tasks by myself and on time.

Task	Date Due
_____	_____
_____	_____
_____	_____
_____	_____
_____	_____

I _____ (*Mom's name*) and I _____ (*student's name*) will do these tasks together and on time.

Task	Date Due
_____	_____
_____	_____
_____	_____
_____	_____
_____	_____

MOM KNOWS BEST

Illustrations from a book can be photocopied and colored, if your child has an art phobia. (Don't forget to give credit in the report.) Computer-generated graphics work well, too.

THE LEAST YOU NEED TO KNOW

◆ Establish a family policy about when homework assignments will be done.

◆ Don't jump in with the answer when you're helping your student on her homework. Give her time to try and figure it out herself.

◆ Homework should reflect the student's efforts. Make sure it's in her own words and is a product of her learning.

Secrets of Successful Studying

One of the most important lessons a student can learn in school is a subject not frequently taught: how to study. Teachers tend to present the material in class and leave the students to master it any way they can. Of course, learning can happen in any number of different ways. What works for one child will not necessarily work for his sister. One of the most helpful things you can do as a parent is encourage your student to figure out what his style of learning is. Once he gets that down, mastering new material will be much easier.

WHAT KIND OF LEARNER?

How we process information affects what we retain. There are visual learners, auditory learners, tactile learners, and kinesthetic learners. Most people are a combination. When you discover how your child learns best, encourage her to use study habits that maximize her innate strengths.

Seeing Is Believing

The visual learner needs to see it in order to process it. She needs to *read* the directions, for example, in order to understand them. If someone is giving the visual learner directions for doing math homework over the phone, this type of student will probably want to write the directions down so she can review them when she gets off the phone.

Hearing Is Understanding

The auditory learner remembers what he hears. He enjoys word play. He retains what he hears when the teacher lectures on a new subject.

Touch, Handle, Manipulate

The tactile learner remembers what she touches, handles, and manipulates. When she studies math, manipulating Cuisenaire rods makes numbers tangible. Most kids are tactile learners.

Move and Experience

The kinesthetic learner needs concrete, hands-on experience to process new information. For example, during a unit on Eskimos, the kinesthetic learner will understand the information best (as well as learn math concepts) by building a model of an igloo. This kind of learner also uses motion and rhythm to absorb material. For example, in trying to remember spelling words, he might develop a rhythm to the syllables in each word.

What Kind of Learner Is Your Child?

This questionnaire, from the book *Bringing Out the Giftedness in Your Child,* by Dr. Kenneth Dunn, Rita Dunn, and Donald Treffinger, will help you determine your child's perceptual strengths. Have your student answer these questions. Stress that there's no right or wrong answer.

	TRUE	FALSE
When I learn something new, I most like to learn about it by:		
1. Reading about it		
2. Hearing a record		
3. Hearing a tape		
4. Seeing a filmstrip (no sound track)		
5. Seeing and hearing a movie (with sound track)		
6. Looking at pictures and having someone explain them		
7. Hearing my teacher tell me		
8. Playing games		
9. Going someplace and seeing for myself		
10. Having someone show me		
The things I remember best are the things:		
11. My teacher tells me		
12. Someone other than my teacher tells me		
13. Someone shows me		
14. I learned on trips		
15. I read		
16. I heard on records or tapes		
17. I heard on the radio		
18. I saw on television		
19. I read stories about		
20. I saw in a movie		
21. I tried or worked on		
22. My friends and I talked about		

What Kind of Learner Is Your Child? (*continued*)	TRUE	FALSE
I really like to:		
23. Read books, magazines, or newspapers		
24. See movies		
25. Listen to records		
26. Make tapes on a tape recorder		
27. Draw or paint		
28. Look at pictures		
29. Play games		
30. Talk to people		
31. Listen to other people talk		
32. Listen to the radio		
33. Watch television		
34. Go on trips		
35. Learn new things with my hands		
36. Study with friends		
37. Build things		
38. Do experiments		
39. Take pictures or make movies/videos		
40. Use typewriters, computers, calculators, or other machines		
41. Go to the library		
42. Trace things in substances like sand or mud		
43. Mold things with my hands		

This questionnaire will help you determine whether your child is primarily an auditory, visual, tactile, or kinesthetic learner.

Record the statements to which your child responded "True" and compare them to the following table to determine your child's dominant perceptual style for learning. A majority of "True" answers in any one column in the table indicates a tendency toward that perceptual style. If there's a somewhat even distribution of "True" answers throughout the four columns, your child probably has equally distributed perceptual learning style preferences.

AUDITORY	VISUAL	TACTILE	KINESTHETIC
2	1	8	8
3	4	21	9
5	5	27	14
6	6	29	21
7	7	35	26
11	8	37	29
12	9	39	34
16	10	40	37
17	13	42	38
18	15	43	39
22	18		
25	19		
30	20		
31	24		
32	28		
36	33		
	41		

Reprinted with permission from Bringing Out the Giftedness in Your Child *by Dr. Kenneth Dunn, Rita Dunn, and Donald Treffinger. New York: John Wiley & Sons, Inc., 1992.*

SIMPLE STUDY TIPS

Testing is a necessary evil in education. It isn't about grades; it's about what your student has learned. Still, the bottom line is that he has to pass the tests in order to move on to the next grade.

Some smart kids are lousy test takers. Others don't have a clue about how to study. In the section that follows, you'll find some tips for helping your student prepare for and take exams.

Ready? Get Organized First

Organizational skills are as important in studying for a test as they are in writing research papers. You can help your child by encouraging him to work steadily, setting goals and due dates for himself as he prepares for a test. On the day the test is announced, have your child develop a study schedule and post it on the bulletin board.

As every mom knows, cramming—waiting until the last minute to study for an exam—is counterproductive. Studying for a test should be review time, not learning-the-subject time. If your child has been doing his homework, keeping up with class assignments, and reviewing new material as it's introduced in class, then when a test is announced, he shouldn't have to do catch-up.

MOM KNOWS BEST

Learning is an ongoing process, not a series of memorized units to be forgotten as soon as the test is over.

Set? Before the Test

Before the test, have your student gather together and organize the materials she will need to study: homework assignments, class notes, outlines, quizzes, and handouts.

After she reviews the material, offer to develop a practice test, or let her write one. Sit down together after she "takes" it and go over the results. Does anything need additional review?

Go! The Day of the Test

Some kids are ready to run out the door on test day with only a few hours of sleep and a jelly doughnut for breakfast. Hold it right there! Moms know that being well rested and eating a balanced breakfast are important to doing well. Encourage your child to go to sleep at a reasonable hour and eat more than pure sugar for her pre-test meal. She'll need to be alert, well rested, and well fed to concentrate during the exam.

ALL IN THE FAMILY

Here's a tried and true method you can teach your child to help her do her best on tests. It has an easy-to-remember acronym: STAR.

♦ *Survey* the test to see which questions can be answered quickly.

♦ *Take time* to read the test directions carefully.

♦ *Answer* the questions you know first, leaving difficult items for last.

♦ *Reread* the questions and your answers to make necessary corrections.

Let your child know that it's best to leave blank any questions she can't readily answer. If she gets hung up on an early question, she may end up rushing through the rest of the exam in order to finish.

After the Test

Review the test results with your child. Talk about which parts were easy and which were difficult. Were incorrect answers the result of careless mistakes or information not studied?

Help your student develop a file for tests and notes. She may need to review the information later for term exams or for understanding more difficult subjects.

MOM KNOWS BEST

High school graduates earn an average of $200,000 more in their lifetime than high school dropouts. College graduates make almost $1 million more.

mom says, slow down!

How does your student study a chapter for a test? Does he read the review questions at the end and then skim the chapter frantically looking for the answers? Hmm. He may be missing something. The following method I recommend takes longer, but it leads to better learning.

1. *Preview the chapter.* Read the introduction to understand what material will be covered in the chapter. Then read the headings, the subheadings, and the summary at the end. Check the illustrations and graphs, because these highlight important information.

2. *Now read the questions.* They will tell you the most important information in the chapter.

3. *Read the chapter carefully.* If you can write in the book, highlight relevant material; otherwise, make flash cards of important facts.

4. *Answer the review questions.* Use the book's index and glossary as guides.

DIVIDE AND CONQUER

As schoolwork becomes more challenging, it's not uncommon for a child to get a bit panicky about the extra responsibility. If your student is not a good reader or seems overwhelmed by the quantity of the material, help her by suggesting that she divide the material into sections and read one section at a time, pausing to rest and "digest." Consider reading together, even alternating sentences, if necessary, until she's used to studying in manageable chunks.

You might want to write a review question or two about each section on flash cards and have her write the answers on the back. Flash cards can be especially helpful for combating test anxiety. If your student reviews her flash cards until the answers are automatic, on the day of the test familiar words and phrases will trigger the answer if she's nervous and blanking out.

STANDARDIZED TEST STRATEGIES

Part of your child's student career will be a series of standardized tests. These have a variety of purposes. Some measure subject competency, others measure natural abilities, and still others measure the school's competency. Some of them your student can study for; others she cannot.

In the latter category are tests designed to determine whether the school's curriculum is teaching certain subjects adequately. These tests are strictly for curriculum planning; they're not included in the student's permanent record.

MOM ALWAYS SAID

Encourage your student to wear a watch on exam days so he can keep track of time and avoid spending too much time on any one question.

Grade Level Competency Tests: No Studying Required

States set their own standards and schedules for measuring student competency in various subjects. For example, in New York, all third graders are given standardized tests to determine whether they're reading at grade level. At this age, most developmental differences will have evened out. The test should pick up significant lags, if they have not already been detected by teachers and parents.

Check with your child's teacher to make sure she's giving students practice competency tests in order to familiarize them with this type of exam. Although your child can't really study for competency tests, becoming familiar with the form should ease test anxiety.

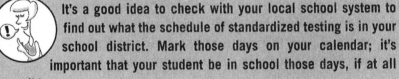

MOM ALWAYS SAID

It's a good idea to check with your local school system to find out what the schedule of standardized testing is in your school district. Mark those days on your calendar; it's important that your student be in school those days, if at all possible.

If your student is absent on a day that a test is given, you'll want to know what provisions are made for her to make it up. One mom, surprised at the low scores her third-grade son received on a standardized reading test, learned that he had been placed in a room by himself to take the test. Without adult supervision, he raced through the exam, performing below his ability. His reading scores improved considerably the following year when he took the test with his class.

Compared to Whom?

Competency test results really need to be read in context. You'll notice that your student's scores will be compared to national averages and also to the scores of other students in your school district. If your community is above average in income and education, the local norm will be different than the national average. For example, a student might score in the 90th percentile in reading when compared to a national average. However, in a high-powered, above-average income and education district, this same student's score might only be in the 80th percentile as compared to other local students.

High School Subject Competency Tests: Please Study

Some states set standards for high school honors classes. There are also advanced placement courses that allow the student to earn college credit in high school. Students *can* study for these kinds of subject competency exams. Most teachers review the material involved in the last few weeks of the semester.

ARCO and Barrons Educational Series publish review guides with practice tests for a variety of subjects.

The Scoop on IQ Tests

Some exams, like the Stanford-Binet or Weschler (commonly referred to as IQ tests), analyze a child's verbal reasoning, quantitative reasoning, abstract/visual reasoning, and short-term memory. They're designed to judge intellectual ability. Some school systems use these tests to screen applicants for talented and gifted programs and magnet schools. (Magnet schools offer a specific curriculum focus, such as math/science, performing arts, or gifted, and draw students from across the school district.)

Controversy continues over the validity of these tests and whether any preparation can improve scores. How your child feels on that particular day and how comfortable she is generally with taking tests can influence her scores.

One mom was surprised when her bright child tested poorly. Then she realized he had taken the test on the day he came down with chicken pox! Subsequent retesting produced significantly higher scores.

MOM KNOWS BEST

If your child's test scores are profoundly different from what you expected, look for an explanation. There shouldn't be any big surprises in testing.

College Prep Tests

Tests like the SAT and ACT are part of the college entrance process. As a rule, kids take these exams twice, first in the spring of their junior year in high school, then again in the fall of their senior year. Colleges will use the best score, which is usually the second one. Just retaking the exam, even without additional studying, tends to improve a student's numbers.

Subject achievement tests (now called SAT II) are part of the admissions process for many colleges. Many schools require applicants to submit the test results of three subject achievement tests. Some students take subject achievement tests at the end of a course when the material is still fresh. For example, a ninth grader completing biology might take his bio achievement exam in the spring of his ninth-grade year, rather than waiting until his junior year, when he would need much more review.

For the SAT I and II and ACT tests, there are review courses, software, and study guides to help your student improve his scores. Talk to your student's guidance counselor about which achievement tests he should take—and when.

MOM ALWAYS SAID

Remember that standardized tests don't test skills like cooperation, determination, creativity, kindness, discipline, or empathy. Keep the tests—and the scores—in perspective.

THE LEAST YOU NEED TO KNOW

◆ Students have different styles of learning and different ways of processing information.

◆ Figuring out how your child learns means you can help him find the best study tools for mastering new information.

◆ Standardized tests are part of the American educational system. Make sure you know what tests your student will take and mark the dates on your calendar.

5

Teachers: The Good, The Bad, The Indifferent

Every mom can remember a teacher who made a difference in her life, good or bad. A good teacher's influence goes beyond whatever subject she teaches, while the damage wreaked by a bad teacher can take years—or a lifetime—to remedy. Unfortunately, you may not have any choice in the teachers your student is assigned to in the course of his educational career. Helping your child maximize the effects of the good teachers and minimize the damage of the mediocre or bad teachers can be a crucial part of his education.

WHEN YOUR CHILD GETS A LEMON

She may be known as the teacher from hell. She yells, plays favorites, and couldn't teach math to Albert Einstein. Or she may be a teacher with mixed reviews—perfect (or at least acceptable) for some kids, a horror show for others.

You need to diagnose the problem before you can plan a solution. Ideally, any problem can be resolved with a concerted effort on the part of the parent, teacher, and student. In reality, you may need to take the lead in finding a creative solution to a difficult problem.

Elementary, My Dear Watson

If your child is having problems with a teacher, a little detective work is needed. Talk to your child. Get him to be as specific as possible about what's bothering him. Is it a misunderstanding? A single incident? A continuing problem?

Has this child had similar problems before? You need to be honest about your child's personality. Does he tend to be overly dramatic? Super sensitive? Does he generally get along with teachers? One mom was candid in her assessment of her two children: "If my older son complains about a teacher I tend to look with a slightly jaundiced eye. He tends to be very sensitive, easily wounded, and quick to gripe. My younger son is very easygoing. When he complains, I know things must be bad because he rarely says a critical word about anyone."

Don't be too quick to judge. On the other hand, even if your child tends to cry wolf, don't tune out too fast. This time there really could be a problem.

What's the Problem?

So what is the problem? Does it have to do with:

- ♦ The teaching style (too fast or too slow)?

- ♦ The subject being taught (a difficult or boring subject)?

- ♦ The teacher (she's mean, unpleasant, or boring)?

These are really different issues. Parents need to know exactly what's behind their student's unhappiness.

The Teacher's Nice But...

Sometimes it's a matter of teaching style. Maybe the teacher is going too fast for your student, or too slow. A good teacher will tailor her approach to meet your child's needs, especially if you or the student can communicate clearly what those needs are. If your student is having trouble keeping up, perhaps additional help can be arranged; if she's bored, you may be able to get her involved in enrichment activities. A teacher is usually sympathetic and willing to work with parents to make sure kids are getting the most they can out of school. One terrific ninth-grade math teacher was known for moving through algebra at the speed of light. Great for the mathematically talented, not so great for the average student. But this teacher was in his room to give extra help every morning at 7 A.M. and after school as well. Kids learned to come in and ask the questions they didn't have time to pose during class.

Education is often a process of trade-offs. Sure it would be great if every teacher met every child's needs, but moms have to figure out how to work with what their kids have been given. And kids need to understand that they can learn from someone they don't particularly like.

A Wicked-Hard Subject

Sometimes the teacher-student tensions are really a cover for "I don't have a clue what's going on in this class." A good teacher should be able to reach even the totally lost student, but at times either one of them may be turned off by attitude. The teacher wants to see enthusiastic students; the student wants to see another subject!

You need to help your student separate the issues. If the problem is with the subject, and not really with the teacher, additional help may be called for, either from the teacher or a tutor (see Chapter 13).

The Teacher Is, Well, Awful

Your child has been assigned a lemon of a teacher. What next?

First, visit the class. You need to observe for yourself what's going on. Send a note asking what day would be best to observe. Most teachers will honor this request, especially if you leave the choice of a date up to them. If not, ask to speak to the principal. Schools should welcome parents.

When you do observe, make notes (unobtrusively) about what you see and hear. You don't need a degree in education to recognize a disorganized, super-critical teacher or one who can't control her class. You'll know it when you see it.

Next, talk to the teacher. Even if your child and everyone else tells you that talking to the teacher won't make any difference, you have to start there anyway. Open with something positive. It will help set the mood for the discussion that follows.

In a calm, nonconfrontational manner, outline your concerns. It's helpful if you make it clear that you're sure that the teacher is concerned, too, even if you're not at all sure she cares! Beginning with something like, "I know we both want Jenny to succeed," makes the two of you appear to be on the same side of the equation. Ask the teacher whether she perceives a problem. She may not agree that there's a problem with your child, or she may have a completely different concern.

Having established a working rapport, you can now turn to the question of how all three parties—the teacher, the student, and the parents—can help resolve the difficulty.

Be forewarned: The teacher may complain about your child. Keep your cool. Gently but firmly get back to the practical issue of how to resolve the problem.

Agree to talk again in two weeks to check progress. Keep notes on the date of the conference, what was said at the meeting, and what decisions were reached. You may need documentation if the situation doesn't improve.

AN UPHILL BATTLE

Before you decide whether to take your complaint up the chain of command, you will want to weigh the risks and benefits of such a step. Parents worry about the effects of going over a teacher's head, and that's reasonable. However, here are some things you should consider.

Worry: What if the teacher takes out her displeasure on my child?

Reality: The bad classroom situation is already penalizing your child. If your student is unhappy and not learning, he's already suffering. Talking to the principal will put the administration on notice that you're carefully watching what happens in the classroom.

Worry: The teacher is a trained professional. Perhaps she does know best.

Reality: The teacher may know educational theory, but her application of it may not be right for your child. Furthermore, she may not be acting in your child's best interests.

Worry: The teacher will accuse me of being overprotective or subjective.

Reality: Of course you're overprotective and subjective about your child—you're supposed to be. Insist, however, that all parties stick to the facts of the case and how they're affecting your child.

Worry: There's no point in complaining. It won't do any good.

Reality: You won't know unless you try. Making your expectations clear to the teacher and administration will force them to focus on the situation.

SO WHERE DO YOU GO NEXT?

In most elementary schools, the person in the chain of command after the teacher is the principal. In high school, start with the chair of the department or your student's guidance counselor or both.

At the meeting, review what was discussed at the teacher conference, what steps you agreed on for remedying the problem, and what the current status is. Ask what steps will now be taken to resolve the dispute. If you're not satisfied with the suggestions, ask for additional remedies.

After the meeting, send a letter to all parties reviewing what happened at the meeting and what were the agreed-upon next steps. It's very important to create a paper trail in case you need to go to the next level.

Bringing Out the Big Guns

You do have two additional weapons, if ordinary methods aren't helping. They are effective, but use them sparingly.

◆ *The doctor card.* If you honestly believe that the classroom situation is intolerable, talk to your pediatrician and, if necessary, a child psychologist. Ask them to write a letter to the school administration detailing their professional concerns about the impact of a bad classroom situation on your child. These experts lend weight to your complaint.

◆ *Power in numbers.* If your child is unhappy with a particular teacher, it's more than likely that other students are, too. Check with other parents and organize yourselves to present a united front to the administration. Again, approach the "powers that be" in a nonconfrontational manner.

Saving Face

The best solution is one where both teacher and principal can live with the outcome without feeling coerced or publicly embarrassed. Using your best people skills to make all parties feel they're acting in the best interests of your child (or at least that they appear to be, for their reputations' sake) will give you credibility you can draw on in the future. It's also likely to make your child's academic life easier.

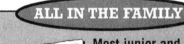

ALL IN THE FAMILY

Most junior and senior high school teachers see an average of 94 students a day.

Time to Request a New Teacher?

If you come to the conclusion that the teacher is incapable of improving or that the classroom situation is harmful, request a change *in writing.* This is the step of last resort because it tends to be hard on the child. Moving into a new class in the middle of the year means making new friends, adjusting to a new learning style, and possibly confronting a hostile environment if the new teacher resents having an additional student. Make an appointment with the new teacher as early as possible in order to work together to ease your child's transition.

Don't bad-mouth the old teacher. Professional loyalty is strong among most educators. Instead, emphasize your willingness to help at home in any way you can to bring your child up to speed, if the new class is at a different point in the curriculum.

PICKING UP THE PIECES

If transferring your child to another class isn't possible, you may have to figure out how to make sure your child continues to learn under difficult circumstances.

Your most important job is to provide your child with emotional support. When a fourth grader complained about his teacher's frequent tirades, one mom refused to make excuses for the teacher's bad behavior. "I told my son that temper tantrums were unacceptable from an adult or a child. I made it clear that he was justified in resenting these outbursts. Even after several parents expressed concern to the teacher about what was happening in the classroom, things didn't change. But at least my son knew that we were supporting him."

You may also have to serve as a substitute teacher. If you believe your student's learning is being seriously compromised, you will either have to tutor him yourself or seek professional tutoring. Try to use the same textbooks that your school uses so you can follow the curriculum.

NAVIGATING THE TEACHER MAZE

Moms know what an incredible impact a good teacher can have on a child's life, so it's understandable that the good ones are in demand. Most school systems have strict rules that limit parents from directly requesting specific teachers. Don't hesitate to speak up, however, if you believe that placement with a certain teacher will affect your child for better or for worse. Remember, you have a unique perspective on your child. That can be a valuable contribution when placement decisions are made.

Generally, you can't come right out and say, "I want Ms. Smith," or even worse, "No way will my child be in Mr. Jones's class." To avoid stepping on toes, savvy moms know they have to speak in code, that is, phrase their requests in language the school will listen to.

◆ *Talk to the teacher you want.* If you think Ms. Smith's third-grade class would be a perfect match for your daughter, approach Ms. Smith informally before class placements are made. Tell her enthusiastically how well you think your daughter would do in her class because she's especially interested in science (if that's Ms. Smith's specialty) or because you think she would do well in an open classroom situation (if that's how Ms. Smith runs her class). The point is to give educational, not personality, reasons for your child to be in her class.

◆ *Talk to your child's current teacher.* Tell him, still in code, about your concerns about placement, emphasizing that you understand how difficult class placements are. After all, teachers and principals must weigh the needs of so many children while trying to create balanced classes. Then list the reasons you believe your child would thrive in a certain kind of classroom. Don't use the names of teachers, but describe the educational atmosphere you believe is best for your child, narrowing your description enough that only one teacher fits the bill.

◆ *Been there, done that....* If one of your older children had a bad experience with a teacher, that's a good reason for requesting a different placement for a younger child. This kind of request is most successful when your family has had a direct experience. Even if you have heard, via the playground grapevine, that a certain teacher is bad news, you really can't use that as grounds for placement. When you've had a personal experience, you have the right to tell those in charge of placement, "We've been down that road before and don't want to go that way again."

◆ *Be wary of putting it in writing.* In this case, you *don't* want to create a paper trail if you can avoid it. You never know when your request may come back to haunt you, especially if your plea is denied. Some schools ask that you direct all placement questions to the principal, rather than to classroom teachers. If possible, however, limit your discussions with the principal to verbal exchanges.

MOM ALWAYS SAID

Pick your battles. You can't go to the mat over every teacher placement, or you lose your clout. Decide which years you absolutely have to take a stand.

CREATING A PARTNERSHIP

Parent-teacher conferences are an opportunity to forge a strong, cooperative relationship with the school, a chance to enjoy basking in your child's progress and an occasion to ask questions or voice concerns. Teachers are an excellent resource for your questions about behavior and development, both in and out of school.

Every teacher should be available to meet with a parent when there's a problem. In addition, most school systems schedule regular parent-teacher conferences, at least in the elementary years. It's your chance to sit down together without interruption and talk about the progress and development of the student.

What a Conference Is Not

There shouldn't be any big surprises at a regularly scheduled parent-teacher conference. If a teacher has observed a serious problem with your student or has a question about behavior, she certainly shouldn't wait for the scheduled conferences to discuss it. By the same token, if you're concerned about what's happening in the classroom, don't hesitate to pick up the phone and call the teacher. Ask for an appointment to meet and discuss your concerns.

At times of significant change in your child's life—if the family is moving to a new house, a grandparent is seriously ill, you or a partner has taken a new job, or you're pregnant—don't wait to share the information with the teacher. You may think you're successfully hiding a stressful situation from your child, but kids are amazingly perceptive and pick up adult "vibes" quickly. Letting your child's teacher know about extra stress in your lives can help her help your child cope.

MOM ALWAYS SAID

Keep your cool at conferences; don't be defensive. You are *not* being graded on your parenting skills. If possible, avoid going into a conference with preconceived ideas. Negative attitudes can block communication.

Both Parents, Please

Ideally, both parents should attend school conferences. This isn't always feasible, of course, but it's important for several reasons. It sends a powerful message to your child that both parents value education and that schooling is a priority, important enough to be included in both parents' schedules. It also sends an important message to the teacher that your family shares child-care responsibilities and considers education a priority.

It also gives the teacher a broader perspective on your child. The two of you—Mom and Dad—have your own understandings and your own ways of relating to your child. Together these can give the teacher a richer understanding of your child's life.

What's on the Agenda?

At the conference, expect to talk about your child's scholastic accomplishments, her academic strengths and weaknesses, her performance in nonacademic subjects (art, music, and physical education), her organizational skills, her classroom participation, her interests, and her peer relationships. What you hear may surprise you, as you discover new sides and interests of the child you send off to school each morning.

Expect Professionalism

The teacher should conduct the conference in a professional manner. This doesn't mean a formal presentation. It does mean that the teacher is prepared (preferably with written notes) to talk specifically about your child.

You're there to discuss your child, not for a generalized overview of the curriculum. The tone should be helpful and encouraging. Even if your child is having difficulties, the teacher should be able to point out areas where he's making progress. You want to see that the teacher has a balanced view of your child and is not focusing exclusively on the problems.

PARENT PREP FOR CONFERENCES

Here are some tips for how to get the most out of the parent-teacher conference:

◆ *Do your homework.* Think about what you want to say or ask about before you go; if it will help you, jot down some notes. Ask your child what's happening in school, and look over recent classwork. Think about your child's learning style (see Chapter 4).

◆ *Be a good listener.* Ask questions about your child's schoolwork and testing results.

◆ *Share your concerns.* Your student's teacher will be most helpful when she's in the loop. Tell her about any significant changes in the household, including a new baby, a divorce, or a death. These can affect your child's behavior and academic performance.

◆ *Follow up.* Reach agreement about what you and the teacher will do if there's a problem, or if you want to encourage a new interest, such as suggesting that your student join the school newspaper in order to reinforce her writing skills. Don't hesitate to ask for a follow-up conference if questions arise after you've had time to think about what was discussed at the conference.

Tone Speaks Volumes

Sometimes not the message but the way it's delivered causes a problem. One experienced school teacher confided that she was nervous when she attended her own children's conferences. She always asked her husband, "So what did you think of the *tone* of the conversation?" Even if all the right words were said, were they believable? Was there any undercurrent or hidden meaning?

Don't hesitate to bring up an uncomfortable topic. You owe it to your child to be honest about what's going on. Choose your words carefully, however, when presenting what appears to be a criticism of the teacher or the school. The last thing you want to do is inflame a difficult situation, and anyway it's quite possible that the teacher is unaware that the child is having a problem. Or there may be a specific reason why he has chosen a certain approach with your student, even if you think it's wrong.

Body language also speaks volumes.

♦ *Make eye contact.* It demonstrates interest and concern. Leaning toward the speaker indicates attentiveness.

♦ *Avoid crossing your arms or legs.* It can indicate a defensive position or anger.

♦ *Pay attention to what's being said.* Sometimes people are so intent on making their own point that they don't listen carefully.

Arrive on Time; Leave Promptly

Respect the conference schedule. Teachers usually schedule several conferences in a row, and a late arrival or delayed departure can throw everyone off. If you know you're going to be late, or if you have to reschedule, call ahead. This shows the teachers that you consider their time as valuable as your own.

Don't hesitate to make another appointment if you feel you need more time or some topics still need to be discussed.

Follow Through with Your Child

Be sure and take the time to discuss the *positive* highlights of the conference with your student. You'll also want to discuss, calmly, any problems or areas in need of improvement. Always begin on a positive note.

VOLUNTEERING PAYS OFF

When moms offer their time, their expertise, and sometimes their money, it pays off for their students.

On a very practical level, the school often needs your help to enrich the class experience. Class trips won't happen unless enough adults are there to supervise. Special projects, like class plays and craft days, frequently need extra assistance to help students manipulate materials or keep things moving along.

ALL IN THE FAMILY

Laurence Steinberg, professor of psychology at Temple University in Philadelphia, reports that according to research, children of parents who volunteer in their youngsters' schools have higher self-esteem and higher grades.

But even if you can't spend time in the classroom, you can volunteer to do what you can do—in the time you have. With each effort, you're sending a powerful message to your child: *Education is important to our entire family*. In fact, it's important enough that Mom and Dad *make time* in their schedule to help.

Here's another intangible benefit from volunteering: Teachers and school directors are human and may well remember who stepped forward when the call for help was sounded. It may mean they listen a little more closely when you ask for a favor or request a special teacher.

Volunteering also gives you the chance to observe the class dynamics. A mother who had been hearing complaints from her daughter about a playground bully was surprised when she finally met the boy and discovered that he was at least 2 inches shorter and 10 pounds lighter than her daughter. Although she knew that her child's frustration and fears were real, she said, "It helped me put the problem in perspective, both for myself and for my daughter. The playground bully, who had been taking on Goliath proportions, could now be reduced to a very human level."

Can You Juggle?

Your child may be singularly unimpressed with—or unaware of—what you do professionally or as a hobby, but schools are delighted when parents share their talents with their students. A mom or dad who writes children's books can talk to students about what that's like. Doctors and dentists can talk about the human body and the care of teeth; firefighters can talk about fire safety. Many jobs are inherently interesting to talk and learn about—and so are many hobbies. One parent who collected model trains invited his child's class to visit his elaborate display. Let your child's teacher know if you have something you'd like to share.

Got No Time

You may not be available to volunteer during school hours, but there are still many ways to be helpful. You could:

- ◆ Make calls as part of a class telephone chain.
- ◆ Volunteer to prepare a class/school newsletter.
- ◆ Head (or assist) a fund-raising effort.
- ◆ Paint or repair school equipment.
- ◆ Arrange a speaker for a parents' meeting.

THE LEAST YOU NEED TO KNOW

- ◆ If a problem arises that your student and her teacher can't work out together, you may need to step in to get the problem resolved. Document your meetings with the teacher; if necessary, meet with the principal and school administration.

- ◆ Do your homework before you go into a parent-teacher conference. Review with your child how things are going in class and ask whether she sees any problems. Don't hesitate to ask the teacher questions or use him as a resource.

- ◆ Volunteer in your child's school. You'll learn a lot about your child just by being in the classroom or on a trip. Your child's school needs your help in order to provide quality educational programs.

6

The Report Card: More Than Just Grades

Ah, report card day—remember? The suspense, the elation, the dismay. Would dinner be a celebration or a confrontation?

Now that we're the grown-ups, we can help our children keep their report cards in perspective and even use them as a learning tool.

WHAT DO REPORT CARDS TELL US?

The first thing to remember about report cards is that they're of limited value. For one thing, all they can really report is past performance. Report cards tell us what our children accomplished during a certain time period, but they can't predict with certainty our child's short- or long-term academic future. *Kids need to understand that a bad report card does not spell lifelong academic failure.*

MOM KNOWS BEST

Before the report card is due, talk to your child about what he expects to see. Once the grades are in, discuss how closely his expectations met reality.

Report cards are also limited in *what* they measure. There's a lot more to your child than academic skills. Even a perfect report card doesn't guarantee personal success. You can flunk math without failing as a human being; you can also be extremely bright and lack the interpersonal skills necessary to live comfortably in society.

One thing a report card should not be is a total shock, or even a surprise. If you've been talking frequently with your student about what she's learning in school and keeping tabs on homework and test results, the report card should confirm what you basically know. A significant difference between grade expectations and realities is cause for a talk with the student, and perhaps the teacher.

MOM ALWAYS SAID

If your child fails a subject and you haven't had any advance warning about it, contact the principal. Parents should be notified if their child is in danger of failing a subject while there's still time to salvage the grade.

GET A GRIP ON GRADES

School systems use different grading methods. Some elementary schools, especially for the lower grades, prefer to issue narrative reports, without any letter or numerical grades. In school systems that use a conventional letter grade system, the numbers that correspond with the grades are as follows:

Letter Grade	Numerical Value
A+	97 or above
A	93–96
A-	90–92
B+	87–89
B	83–86
B-	80–82
C+	77–79
C	73–76
C-	70–72
D+	67–69
D	65–66
F	Below 65, failing

Grade Point Average	Numerical Value
4.0	95
3.5	90
3.0	85
2.5	80
2.0	75
1.5	70
1.0	65
Below 1.0	Failing

Some schools *weight*, or give extra points, for honors or advanced placement (AP) courses in recognition of the challenge these courses represent. Students taking an honors English class in eleventh grade, for example, may have three points automatically added to their English grade point average, while seniors taking AP English in the same school may have six points added. In this kind of a system, at the end of high school a student could have more than a 100-point average.

Tests + Homework + Class Participation + Effort = Grade

Every teacher calculates grades in his or her own way. Some go by straight arithmetic computation (add up the test grades and then divide by the number of tests); others have such elaborate systems that it would take a math genius to understand them. Others factor in homework and class participation, making test scores 50 percent of the final grade, for instance, and homework and class participation 25 percent each.

Some teachers and some courses are more difficult than others. You may need to adjust your child's (and your own) grade expectations accordingly. But academic challenges are good for kids and respected by colleges. If your student has the opportunity to take an honors or advanced placement class, it's worth it, even if her grades are slightly lower. She'll get credit for challenging herself.

ALL IN THE FAMILY

One ninth-grade English teacher used a grade as an incentive for continued good work. She "loaned" a struggling student two points so he could reach his goal of making the third-quarter honor roll. Next quarter, he more than made up the "loan" of points.

E for Effort?

What role should effort play in grades? Should the average student who works very hard be rewarded for her effort even if her performance is below average? Or should grades simply reflect performance?

The ideal answer is probably somewhere in the middle, but it's up to the individual teacher to figure out how she will factor effort into her grading and communicate that decision to her students.

MOM KNOWS BEST

If parents are divorced, barring a court order to the contrary, noncustodial parents have a right to see their children's school reports. Talk to the teacher to find out how you can receive a copy of your child's grades.

Incentive? Or Bribe?

Some moms like to use an "incentive program," rewarding good grades with money. Education specialists tend to worry about this practice. It's thought that offering an incentive—or let's be honest, a bribe—for good grades blunts a student's self-motivation and puts the emphasis on the grade instead of on learning.

It's a great idea to recognize progress and achievement. Rather than put a dollar value on a specific grade point average, though, why not acknowledge the child's accomplishment with a treat or an outing? When your child brings a grade up a notch or two, or when the teacher has made an especially kind remark on the report card, celebrate with your student by doing something fun together.

BAD NEWS, GOOD NEWS

So the report card brought some disappointment. You'll want to talk with your student about strategies for improvement. But first, BEGIN WITH THE POSITIVE. Absolutely everyone, regardless of age, responds better to a conversation that begins with a compliment. You might discuss the progress you've seen over the year, the good mark in a favorite subject, or the teacher's comments on cooperation. Don't just zero in on the problems.

Your student is probably more disappointed than you about a bad grade, even if he doesn't seem to show it. He may be pretending grades don't matter, because then it won't matter if his grades are good or bad. He can't be a failure if he isn't invested in the process, right? But secretly he probably feels badly about it.

MOM KNOWS BEST

If the report card was very disappointing, have your student make a fresh start. Have her clean out her locker, get clean notebooks, and get organized for a new beginning.

Talk with Your Child

Cool it, Mom. This is not the time for yelling and recriminations. No matter how discouraged, frustrated, and angry you might be, you need to keep your head.

When everyone's feeling calm, ask your child to bring out her homework and tests. By reviewing the subject material, you may be able to see what went wrong. For example, if she had difficulty understanding the subject when it was first introduced, her problems may have snowballed by the end of the quarter as the material grew more difficult. If she wasn't keeping up with her homework, then she may have been penalized even if her test scores were good. Talk it through with her and see whether you can work out positive solutions together. Be respectful.

What Else Is Going On?

Here's how to put the report card into perspective:

- *Look at the big picture.* Is the problem with a single grade, or is your student struggling in all her subjects?

- *What's the trend look like?* Have the grades been steadily declining all year, or is this particular quarter an aberration? Is a problem at home or a social problem affecting her grades? Did she miss school because of illness? Did she begin a new sport or win a role in a play? These can be time-intensive activities.

- *Compare the current report card to previous years.* Do you see a pattern? One student often had a third-quarter slump: His grades would go down around April each year (he called it "schoolitis"), and then rebound during the last quarter after a pep talk from Mom. Others may start off slow each year as they adjust to the new teacher and then get stronger as the year progresses.

♦ *Talk to the teacher.* You need the teacher's input into what happened this quarter. He can probably suggest strategies for improvement. He may also reassure you that your student has already begun taking action, or that she seems to be getting a handle on the material.

Trust your judgment. One mom was worried when her normally straight-A seventh grader brought home a report card full of Bs. Not a bad report card by any stretch of the imagination, and not one to set off alarm bells with teachers. But this mom knew this wasn't her daughter's usual standard. She did a little probing and found that the social pressures of junior high were having their effect.

It's not being overly grade conscious to recognize that a report card can gauge how things are going in your child's life. In this case, the mom was able to help her daughter through a difficult social situation that was affecting her schoolwork.

MOM KNOWS BEST

It's more important that your child is an *educated* student than a straight-A student. Remember: The focus should be on learning, not the grade.

What Are You Going to Do About It?

First, talk with your child about what action will help her improve her grades. Does she need a tutor? (See Chapter 13.)

Is a physical disability affecting her learning? (Make an appointment for vision or hearing checkups.) Perhaps she needs to reorder her priorities or improve her study habits.

Follow up with the teacher and your child. Make an appointment to talk to the teacher in two weeks to see how things are going, and keep in close communication with your child about school. You don't want to micromanage her academic career, but you do want to stay on top of any academic problems.

The Grade's Unfair

What if your child insists that his teacher is simply unfair in how she grades?

♦ *Listen carefully to his complaints.* Has he been having difficulty with the teacher and her grading system all semester? Are other children in the class similarly affected? Check with other parents.

♦ *Suggest that he talk to the teacher first.* Encouraging your child to resolve problems on his own is a mark of respect. It makes him feel that he has an important role in his school career. It also helps establish a line of communication between the teacher and the student. This is helpful, no matter how the problem is resolved. One student, frustrated over an English grade, sat down and talked with her teacher, one-on-one, for the first time in the semester. Although the grade didn't change, the student believed that she had a better idea of what criteria was used to determine grades and how to improve for next semester.

♦ *Follow up with an appointment with the teacher.* If your student still believes that the grade is unfair, it's time for the grown-ups to talk. Ask the teacher about the range of grades in the class and exactly how she computed your child's grade. Then, if you're still dissatisfied, make an appointment with the principal.

No Matter What: I Love You

It's easy to get caught in the grade trap. Kids worry about how their parents are going to react to their report cards. Temper your reactions—good and bad.

It's fine to praise your child for an impressive report—one that reflects your child's effort—but you never want a kid to believe that your relationship is affected by how well he does in school. Kids can worry that your love is contingent on their maintaining a high average.

Sure you get disappointed when the grades aren't good, especially if you think your child hasn't been trying hard. But no matter what the report card says, Mom, make sure your child knows that your love is unconditional.

There Must Be Some Mistake!

Actually, mistakes can happen, as one mom ruefully discovered. When her seventh grader's report card arrived in the Saturday morning mail, she was indignant at the science grade. The kid kept protesting that he was equally surprised, that the grade was 10 points lower than he expected. Mom lectured about the need for new study habits and restricted TV viewing. But on Monday morning, during a hasty parent-teacher phone conference, the teacher was equally surprised at the grade. Apparently, the wrong mark had been entered on the student's report card. The seventh grader had been right about his grade!

MOM ALWAYS SAID

If you think there's been an error, check it out. Otherwise, the incorrect grade will remain.

THE COMMENT PAGE

Kids are more than the sum of their grades. In addition to evaluating how your student is performing in math, science, and reading, the report card will attempt to assess her emotional and social development. This part of the report card is just as important as the grade sections, if not more so. It evaluates your child as a student, compared to norms for her age. Expect the teacher to address questions like:

◆ Does the student work independently?

◆ Is she conscientious about her assignments, turning them in neatly and on time?

◆ Is she willing to challenge herself?

- Does she work well with other classmates?
- Does she participate in class discussions?

"F" for Poor Behavior

If your child's teacher complains on the report card about his classroom behavior, call for an appointment to talk (either by phone or in person). You and the teacher need to get to the root of the problem and develop strategies for improvement. Not only is poor behavior disruptive to the class, it affects your child's own academic performance.

Teachers are human. If your child gets a reputation for being difficult, he's less likely to get the kind of attention—positive feedback—that he needs. It can become a self-fulfilling expectation. Johnny is known to be a difficult child, and then continues to be one. This kind of a reputation can follow a child throughout his academic career.

Following Up

If the teacher has not been in communication with you during the quarter to discuss your child's difficult behavior, and the first you hear of it is when you get the report card, you need to strengthen the lines of communication between home and school. If necessary, talk with the teacher and agree on a method of checking in on a weekly basis until the problem is under control. In the meantime, here are some things to work on:

- *Find out what's wrong.* You need to figure out what's happening in the classroom and why. Something very simple could be tipping your child's behavior in the wrong direction. Perhaps sitting next to a best friend encourages in-class talking. Just changing seats may help. Perhaps she's frustrated by the subject and acting out her frustration. Getting academic help may help resolve the problem. Once you know what the problem is and why it's happening, you can determine a strategy for change.

- *Make your expectation of good behavior clear.* Let your child know that you will be monitoring her behavior through the teacher.

If the misbehavior is severe, you might enlist the teacher to write a daily note in your child's assignment book letting you know whether she behaved in class that day. It's a fine line, of course. You don't want your child to feel that she can't move without being judged; on the other hand, she has to understand that disruptive behavior will not be tolerated.

♦ *Reward good behavior.* Not in dollars and cents—that's counterproductive. For an elementary student, try a chart with stars for each day of a good report, with perhaps an ice cream cone to celebrate a full week of good behavior. For an older student, a simple check mark on the calendar and a movie at the end of the week is probably more appropriate. Don't mortify your child by treating him as if he were three years younger, even if his behavior strikes you as immature. Positive feedback is always more productive than negative.

THE PERMANENT RECORD

Your child's permanent school record contains her standardized test scores and copies of her report cards. It can also include reports from members of the school team (speech and hearing teacher, reading specialist, social worker, school nurse, or counselor).

The school may use the information in these records to make academic decisions about a child. For example, the results of standardized tests may be used to determine grouping for advanced math classes. You want to be sure that the information in the record is correct. For example, pertinent medical information that affects your child's academic performance should be included in the file.

FERPA Guarantees Access

You have a right to see your child's permanent record. The Family Educational Rights and Privacy Act (FERPA), also known as the Buckley Amendment, guarantees every parent and guardian the right to review their child's official school record. This file accompanies your child from elementary school to middle school to high school.

If you believe the record contains an error or unjustified information, you can request that it be removed. If the school refuses, you can request a hearing on the issue. You can also add your own letter of correction to the file.

Check Out the Full Record

Be sure to check more than the standardized test scores. Teachers can include negative comments about behavior in the permanent record and so influence future classroom experiences. When your child changes schools (from elementary to middle school, for example, or if you move), the permanent record may be the only way a new teacher can judge your child—until she gets to know him. If she begins the new relationship having been told that this is a "difficult child," it starts the year off on the wrong foot.

Checking your child's permanent record regularly gives you an opportunity to correct errors before they can do damage. If possible, encourage the teacher who has written the comment in the file to remove it. Explain the potential damage this kind of comment can do to a child, that it's neither constructive nor helpful. If the teacher won't change or withdraw the comment, add your own letter of correction to the file.

THE LEAST YOU NEED TO KNOW

- ◆ Report card grades should not come as a surprise. Keep on top of your student's progress throughout the year.

- ◆ Keep grades in perspective. Even if your child's grades are disappointing, separate academic performance from a judgment of him as a person. Kids need to know that even flunking a class isn't going to change how much you love them.

- ◆ If your student receives a disappointing grade, talk to your child and her teacher about what went wrong. Agree to keep in close contact over the next few weeks to monitor progress.

- ◆ Parents have a right to see their child's permanent school record. Make sure the information it contains is accurate.

Read for Success

Moms bug their kids to read because, in the words of the popular slogan, "Reading is fundamental." In order to succeed in school, at the very minimum your child has to be reading at grade level. The best students are invariably good readers, especially when it comes to the upper grades, where instruction is heavily dependent on independent reading and learning. Making sure that your child can and does read is a crucial step in raising a good student.

READING AT GRADE LEVEL...AND BEYOND

At your parent-teacher conference, you may be told that your child is reading at grade level. What does that mean?

Say your fourth grader's reading score is 5.2. That means that compared to a national cross section of fourth graders, she reads like students who are in the second month of fifth grade. That sounds terrific, but don't forget to check the average score of students in your district. An above-average score for the nation may be average or even below average for your district. (See Chapter 4 on how to interpret standardized test scores.)

What do these scores mean for your child, practically speaking? Will they be used to determine her placement in classroom reading groups? In that case, an unrealistically low score—perhaps she wasn't feeling well the day the test was administered—might land her in a lower reading group than her skill level calls for. Make sure her score really reflects her ability.

MOM ALWAYS SAID

 Trust your judgment. If you don't think your child's reading scores are an accurate reflection of her competence, talk to her teacher.

Not at Grade Level

Just as some kids walk before they're a year old and others wait until they're 14 months or older, so there are students who struggle with reading before beginning to soar. Accept developmental differences, up to a point.

If your child is in the lowest reading group in his class, however, you want to know what steps are being taken to improve his reading skills.

♦ *Ask for your child to be tested.* Educational psychologists can administer a battery of tests to determine whether a learning disability could be involved. (See Chapter 13 for more on learning disabilities.)

♦ *Request remedial help for your child.* If it's a small problem, a little one-on-one time with a reading specialist may give your child the boost she needs to start reading on her own. A learning disability, on the other hand, may require long-term help. Schools are required by law to provide help for students who have been diagnosed with learning disabilities.

♦ *Work with your child at home.* Needless to say, this can be a touchy one. If tutoring your child at home creates constant family tension, back off. It's hard to be both mother and teacher, and your child needs her parent first.

♦ *Hire a tutor.* If it's economically feasible, the additional rein-
forcement a qualified tutor provides can make a significant
difference in your child's progress. (See Chapter 13 for where
to find a tutor.)

MOM ALWAYS SAID

Two-thirds of American high school seniors read for less
than an hour a day. One-third of American high school
seniors don't read any books outside of school assignments.

POWER READING

The best way to strengthen reading skills is to read. Bernice E.
Cullinan says in her book, *Read to Me: Raising Kids Who Love to Read:*
"In reading, like so many other things, practice makes perfect...
The more you read, the better you read. The better you read, the
more you enjoy it. The more you enjoy it, the more you want to
read."

So how do moms get their kids to read? Here are 10 tips that
work:

1. *Offer a variety of reading materials.* Take out 10, even 20 books
   from the library every time you visit so that your child has
   plenty of choices. Give her a subscription to a magazine
   geared toward her interests (fashion, sports, entertainment,
   computers...). Offer her the newspaper every day. Whether
   she reads the front page, the sports pages, Ann Landers, or the
   comics, she's reading.

2. *D.E.A.R.* Establish a Drop Everything and Read time for your
   family—20 minutes after dinner and before TV, maybe—when
   everyone in the family sits down and reads. That means you
   too, Mom! Newspaper, magazine, books, anything—just so
   long as you read.

3. *Give positive feedback for reading.* Let your child know that you're
   proud that she reads, just as you're proud of her athletic accomplishments or academic achievements. Reward her with some
   one-on-one time when you talk about what she's reading.

4. *Never use reading as punishment.* Children should never associate reading with bad behavior.

5. *Practice what you preach.* You need to make time to read in your own life, Mom. Kids model reading behavior.

6. *Subscribe to interesting magazines.* Offering a range of reading materials, including popular and current events magazines, is a good way to encourage interest in reading.

7. *Give (and ask for) books as gifts.* Giving books as gifts demonstrates that you consider them something special and wonderful.

8. *Read what your child is reading.* Sharing books makes it easier to have conversations about what your child is reading. It also tells your child that you respect her choices in literature. Some moms like to read aloud with their children, alternating chapters (she reads to you, you read to her); other families read independently, but simultaneously. Whatever works.

9. *Continue to read aloud to your child even when she's an independent reader.* Reading aloud is about more than books. It's important one-on-one time with your child. Depriving your child of that special time may seem like punishment for learning to read. Most children, until they are about 12 years old, are better at listening to stories than they are at reading. They are also more sophisticated listeners than they are readers. You'll be able to read *Wind in the Willows* to your daughter long before she can get through it by herself. This is a great way to build vocabulary and grammar—not to mention families.

10. *Read what's interesting.* So what if it's easy? Not every book your child reads has to be great literature. Don't moms also like to read mysteries, romance novels, and cookbooks? The point is to encourage reading.

MOM KNOWS BEST

With elementary-school kids, offer a later bedtime in exchange for independent reading. Let them read in bed for half an hour before turning out the light.

WHAT ABOUT THOSE CLASSICS?

Classic children's literature like *Treasure Island* or *Tom Sawyer* may already be part of your student's English curriculum. Whether they are or not, you might find yourself wishing that your kids would read "real books" like these instead of the *Goosebumps* and *Babysitters Club* series they're so enthralled with. Keep in mind, though, that classic literature can be hard literature. Many kids—and many adults, too—find these books slow going. The 19th-century language is very difficult, and the sentence structure is complex. Here are some tips for helping your kids read and enjoy these more challenging books:

◆ *Read them together.* Your child may need your help interpreting the language and putting the story in its historical context.

◆ *Watch the movie or read the Cliffs Notes or the illustrated comic book.* Your child may find it easier to get into a difficult book if she can "preview" what will happen. None of these media are a substitute for the real thing, but don't feel you can't use them to help your child through a difficult assignment.

◆ *Use the book as a springboard for discussion.* Discuss the themes of the book and explore its relevance today. Reading *Tom Sawyer* or *Huck Finn* is a great opportunity to examine the lives of children yesterday and today and current attitudes about race and women.

The Rule of Thumb

Is the book your child has selected too difficult for him to read alone? The Parent Institute, an educational publishing house, suggests that you try the "rule of thumb." Have your child read one page of the book aloud, holding up a finger for every word he doesn't understand. If he holds up four fingers and his thumb before he gets to the bottom of the page, the book is probably too difficult. Try reading it together.

For struggling readers, make sure the type is large and clear and that the pages have plenty of white space. Also, the illustrations should explain the text.

Mom, What Does This Word Mean?

Reading shouldn't be a dictionary exercise. If your student asks what a word means while he's reading, tell him. Don't insist he look it up or sound it out, or he'll quickly come to think of reading as a chore. As he experiences success in reading, he'll learn to use context to define a word.

If you're not sure whether your student is reading for meaning or just decoding the words, ask him to explain what he's reading to you. What or who is the main point in the sentence or paragraph? What's going on, and why?

Help him distinguish between important and extraneous details. Which are just there to add richness to the story, and which are essential? Teach him to look for clues in the way sentences are ordered in the paragraph. Does the most important information come first?

ENCOURAGING THE RELUCTANT READER

Moms sometimes worry when their kids seem to read anything but books. And, the books they do choose don't always seem to have a lot of cultural significance. It may comfort these moms to learn that Charles Dickens was as popular in his day as R.L. Stine is in ours. (But did you know Dickens's novels came out in serial form in the newspapers of the time?)

Okay, so maybe popular fiction series like *Goosebumps* or *Animorphs* will never be mistaken for great literature. Still, they do capture kids' imaginations and turn them on to reading. From reading *Goosebumps,* your child might be willing to try science fiction by writers of the caliber of Isaac Asimov and Ray Bradbury. Mystery lovers might move from Nancy Drew to O. Henry or Edgar Allan Poe.

MOM KNOWS BEST

Encourage your child to read at odd moments—in the bath, in the doctor's waiting room... Keep a tote bag full of reading materials in the car; get the kid in the habit of grabbing a book along with her coat.

Books for Reluctant Readers

Many moms (and lots of dads) remember reading comic books when they were young, but keep hoping their kids have better taste. Still, as one mom finally decided, "Better to read comic books than nothing at all!"

Some kids prefer a nonfiction book that lets them read a page or two and pick up some interesting information without committing to a whole chapter or an entire book.

When choosing books for your reluctant reader:

◆ *Cater to her interests.* If she likes sports, look for books on sports. Don't forget biographies of sports stars and sports annuals of team statistics.

◆ *Find books that relate to her life.* Is she having problems with friends or a move to a new neighborhood? Reading novels that relate to her situation can be very helpful. If you can't think of the right book, ask a children's librarian for help.

◆ *Try joke books.* These are often a hit. You may have to put up with some very tired jokes, but you'd be amazed how well they encourage reading.

◆ *Work with the children's librarian.* Your child is not the first reluctant reader your local librarian has met. She may have suggestions for books that have captured other kids' interests.

◆ *Accept comfort over proficiency.* You're trying to entice your child to read. Quantity is better than quality—at least for the short term. Suggest books that are below her reading proficiency so she can feel good about finishing several. She'll know when she's ready to try harder books.

◆ *Poetry can be magic.* Remember how your child loved the verbal silliness of Dr. Seuss? Silly, spooky, or lyrical, poetry can often capture a child's imagination when books don't. Look for poetry books aimed at young readers. Shel Silverstein is a perennial favorite for kids.

ONCE MORE, WITH FEELING...

Family story hour is important even after your children learn to read. To capture your child's interest, learn to read aloud with expression. Make the book come alive. Your child will learn the beauty and richness of language as he listens.

Read sitting up, and make sure it's a book you both like. Make frequent eye contact, especially when you want to let something sink in or when the language seems difficult. Your child's reactions should help guide your style.

Define hard words as you go along without waiting to be asked. Stopping too often to ask, "Do you know what such-and-such means?" can spoil the pace of the story. On the other hand, there's nothing wrong with pausing to exchange comments or answer questions from time to time. In fact, it's a great sign!

Don't worry about setting an arbitrary quota of pages to be read each night. Instead, play things by ear. The goal is for your child to be engaged. So *have fun!* Modify your voice as you take on different characters—loud, soft, deep, high, laughing, angry, serious... Enjoy yourself, and your enthusiasm will be infectious.

SEEING TO READ

Occasionally a reluctant reader turns out to have vision problems. Even if your child has passed the vision screening test given at school, you may want to have her eyes tested if she exhibits any of these symptoms:

◆ An eye that turns in or out and does not seem to be in alignment with the other

◆ Red eyes or lids, frequent tearing, or encrusted eyelids

◆ Frequent squinting at close or distant targets

Your child may complain of one or more of the following:

◆ Headaches, especially in the region of the forehead or eyes

◆ Print blurring after a short period of time

◆ A burning or itching sensation in the eyes after reading or writing

◆ Double vision

While reading, your child may:

◆ Skip or reread lines repeatedly

◆ Frequently leave words out

◆ Often use a finger to keep his or her place in the material

While writing, your child may:

◆ Frequently repeat letters within words

◆ Become frustrated when copying material from a book or a chalkboard

Physical signs of problems during reading or writing include:

◆ Closing or covering one eye

◆ Rubbing the eyes

◆ Excessive blinking while writing or reading but not at other times

◆ Awkward reading or writing posture (Your child may slump over, nose nearly touching the page; frequently change the distance between his or her eyes and the page; or turn his or her head while reading across the page.)

Young children write or draw all over the page while they are developing motor control and mastering the conventions of writing, but an older child who does one or more of the following may have an eye problem:

♦ Goes over the lines when writing on a lined page

♦ Writes with a ragged left margin

♦ Writes, draws, or does math problems crookedly on the page

Reprinted with permission of Caroline Beverstock and the International Reading Organization from the booklet, Your Child's Vision Is Important.

READING: THE GENDER GAP

Ray Messing, a children's librarian and mom of two boys, thinks reading isn't valued in our society, especially among older boys. "Girls tend to read more. Our society accepts it more. It's not very 'in' for boys to read. Most boys feel pressured to achieve in sports. While boys will readily talk about their batting average, I don't know that being a serious reader is something that boys brag about. In contrast, as they grow older, it's more acceptable for a girl to shun athletics in favor of reading. There are more role models of women who read. Research has shown that women read books, while men read 'non-books' such as newspapers and periodicals."

Of course, parents need to buck the trend of non-reading boys and couch potato girls. Discover the books that will capture your son's interests; encourage your daughter to read *and* be physically active.

ALL IN THE FAMILY

According to a report from The National Assessment of Educational Progress, The California Reading Program, boys between the ages of 8 and 10 rank outdoor sports first in terms of fun; reading finished sixth. Girls in the same age group ranked reading first and outdoor sports second.

Girls Like...

Most elementary and junior high school girls like "problem" books. In these types of novels, the main character has to resolve a major personal crisis, such as the lack of boyfriends, obesity, or moving to a new city. Feminine stereotypes are often rampant in older novels. Talk to your daughters about what they are reading, reminding them that when it comes to stereotypes, life should not imitate art.

Offer alternatives that show girls as independent and resourceful. For great books that feature strong female characters, check out the offerings at Athena Books, an online bookstore that can be reached at AthenaBook@aol.com.

Athena founder Kim Prather Strazis, mom of two girls, established these criteria for what she would include in her virtual bookstore:

◆ The main character of the book must solve a problem or achieve a goal through ingenuity or strength of character.

◆ The main characters must not achieve their goals at others' expense.

◆ The book must not involve bartered spouses. No "the man who can wrestle the biggest rhino gets to marry the princess" scenarios.

The store also offers plenty of books featuring male characters. "When I looked at these lovely books all in a row," remarks Strazis, "I was struck by how multi-cultural this collection is, and I was delighted! It shows that people are good, brave and strong, no matter what their color, nationality or gender."

Some moms keep their daughters reading with mother-daughter book clubs. Talking about books is a great way to keep the conversation going between generations. *The Mother-Daughter Book Club,* by Shireen Dodson and Teresa Barker, offers guidelines for starting your own group. Of course, there's no reason why moms and sons, or dads and their kids, can't join or form their own book clubs.

Boys Like...

Elementary and junior high school boys tend to prefer biographies, science fiction, mysteries, and fantasies. Sports books are often a big hit, and so are sports magazines and the sports pages of the newspaper. Yes, I know it feels like gender stereotyping, but if your son doesn't like books, these resources may at least get him reading. Try reading along with your son so you can discuss issues such as gender stereotyping or sports hype around Super Bowl time.

ALL IN THE FAMILY

A librarian mom remembers the one book that her non-reading son did read "cover to cover." It was a children's book on human sexuality. After finishing the tome in one evening, the boy took the book off the shelf the very next day and declared, "That was good. I'll think I'll read it again."

THE LEAST YOU NEED TO KNOW

◆ Continue to read aloud to your student even after she's a competent reader.

◆ Classic literature may be difficult to read because of the complex language and sentence structure. Read along with your child. Leave time for questions and comments.

◆ If your child continues to have problems reading, insist the school run a complete evaluation to rule out learning disabilities. Have your child's vision checked as well.

◆ Older boys often get the message that reading is something that girls do. Make sure that your children, girls and boys, understand that "Reading is fundamental."

The Write
Stuff

The original three R's of education were reading, 'riting, and 'rithmetic—an early example of invented spelling! Elementary, junior high, and high school curricula are far more complex than they were in those days, but writing is still basic. Students need to be able to express themselves coherently, logically, and thoughtfully. And on a very practical level, teachers need to be able to read their students' handwriting in order to assess whether they understand the material and can express their thoughts and ideas in writing.

READ TO WRITE

Writing and reading are closely related. Ask incoming kindergarten students if they know how to read, and most will answer no. But ask those same children if they know how to write, and the answer might well be an enthusiastic "yes!" Kids learn early that the scribbles and drawings they produce tell a story, just like the words on the pages of their books. Writing and reading are equal forms of communicating meaning.

That's why, since your student entered school, her teachers have been encouraging her to write (or dictate) her thoughts. As she progresses through school, her reading and writing skills become even more interrelated. Good writers are good readers. They learn writing techniques from the authors they read. The more your child reads, the better her writing will become.

One of the advantages of continuing to read aloud to children, even after they've become competent readers, is that they discover the rich possibilities of written language. As the books become more sophisticated, so too will the language. And as she reads more complex material, her own writing will become more sophisticated.

MOM ALWAYS SAID

Spoken language is more informal, the sentence structure is less complicated. Written language uses punctuation to define meaning; it has to be more precise because there's no voice inflection or body language to define what the speaker is trying to say.

WRITING TEACHES THINKING

Teaching children how to write well means getting them to think about communication, about expressing ideas and information so that they're truly understood. The heart of good communication, in turn, is organization. Putting their thoughts on paper forces writers of all ages to focus and order what they've learned. As your child builds her writing skills, she's also building her ability to think analytically and make creative connections.

Chances are your child has spent a lot of class time mastering the techniques of expository writing. Putting these skills into practice, however, often takes place at home, when she's working on book reports and papers. In the section that follows, I'll review the principles of well-organized writing so that you in turn can be a resource for your student writer.

In the Beginning...

Writing begins with an idea. Teachers use the technique of the topic sentence because it forces the student to focus and clarify before she even puts pen to paper. The first task of a writing project, then, whether fiction or nonfiction, is to develop a topic sentence that defines what the project is. Once your writer has a good topic sentence, she can proceed to facts or images that support her idea. Bingo: She's thinking analytically. You can help your student develop the art of the topic sentence by having her identify topic sentences in the books and articles she reads.

Next, Please

Step two is planning. Some teachers require students to write a formal outline for term papers or reports. Even if your child's teacher is relaxed about outlines, the child will benefit from taking time to sketch a plan for the paper before he begins writing. The plan should include a list of the facts and ideas with which he will support his topic sentence and numbers to indicate the order in which they will be presented. Suggest that he brainstorm the list first, then take time to think it over and order it so the most important information comes first.

I'd Like to Thank...

When the project is a research report, the teacher will almost certainly require a bibliography or footnotes to show what resources were used to create the paper. At this stage of your child's education, you may want to add a style manual to your home library. Also available as software, it gives the correct forms for references and citations, along with useful guidance on everything to do with writing well.

"IT WAS A DARK AND STORMY NIGHT"

Sometimes the easiest assignments are straightforward, factual reports. Trying to encourage the "creative" side of the student writer can result in miserable cries of, "I can't," "I don't have anything to say," or, "I hate poetry!" What's a mom to do?

The best-selling author Mary Higgins Clark, mother of five, says that she begins many of her novels with the question, "What if?" For kids facing writer's block, this isn't a bad place to begin. Here are some other tips to stir the creative juices:

◆ Write a popular fairy tale from the point of view of another character. How does the Big Bad Wolf view Red Riding Hood's story?

◆ Write a sequel to a favorite story.

◆ Use a real-life incident in the newspaper as a jumping-off point for a fictional story.

MOM KNOWS BEST

Parents and Children Together, an online magazine (also available in print) is a great place for kids and parents to submit stories and articles for publication. Check out the Web site at http://www.indiana.edu/~eric_rec/fl/pcto/menu.html.

THE THREE R'S (NO, THE OTHER ONES)

The Parent Institute, an educational publisher, recommends that a student remember the three R's when beginning a writing project: wRite, Revise, and Review. First, *write* the ideas down on paper. Second, *revise* punctuation, grammar, and spelling. And third, *review* the final copy for typos and errors.

When the final copy is to be handwritten, teach your student how to insert carets for inadvertently omitted words and how to cross out neatly. You know the hysteria that can develop when a mistake is discovered in a final, handwritten copy. Reassure your student that the teacher will understand if she makes her corrections neatly.

ANSWER THE QUESTION, PLEASE

As the student gets older, exams will often include questions that call for long, expository answers. With these kinds of exams, the most important thing to remember is to read the instructions carefully before beginning. Remind your student to look for the verb the teacher uses in the question as the clue to the answer. For example:

- **"Compare** *the Revolutionary War with the War of 1812"* means "Find the similarities between the two events."

- **"Contrast** *the Revolutionary War with the War of 1812"* means "Find the differences between the two events."

- **"Comment** *on the role of the Monitor and Merrimack in the Civil War"* requires the student to explain the impact and meaning of an issue or event.

- **"Justify** *the bombing of Hiroshima in World War II"* means "Defend the action."

- **"Criticize** *the bombing of Hiroshima"* means "Express an opinion based on facts."

Some essay questions require the student to do more than one of these: "Compare and contrast the Revolutionary War with the War of 1812."

MY MOTHER, MY MUSE

You can encourage your child's writing abilities by incorporating the written word into home life. Here are some ways to do that:

- *Letter to the editor.* Whether your local paper is the *Weekly Gazette* or the *New York Times,* your child can use her words for effect. Have her write a letter to the editor, taking a stand on an issue that affects kids or reporting on school events. If her letter gets printed, she will really see the power of her words.

- *Freebies for words.* Invite your child to write to a toy company (or some other company he cares about) with a testimonial, complaint, or suggestion. Sometimes companies include coupons for free products in their responses. Wow! Writing works!

- *Pen pals.* Nowadays, a lot of pen pals are really e-pals—e-mail correspondents, that is. E-mail or snail mail if your child can start a regular correspondence with a child her age, it's great communication practice.

- *Published writer.* Several magazines publish children's writing or hold writing contests. *Stone Soup* and *Seventeen,* for example. Oh, and check out KidPub, an online 'zine. The Web site is: http://www.kidpub.org/kidpub. (Omit the final period when typing the address.)

- *Family listmaker.* Appoint your child to the office of Family Listmaker for the week. She's in charge of shopping lists, appointment lists, gift lists, etc. It will help her (and you) get organized.

- *Script writer.* Invite your student to write a play script; then mount a production of it. Videotape it for posterity.

- *Dear Diary.* Keeping a journal is a great way to encourage writing. One mom gave her daughter a diary and also bought one for herself. Before bed is journal-writing time for both—and sometimes they share their entries.

- *Family letter.* A note to the extended family doesn't have to wait for the holidays. Your writer can be the official monthly newsbearer. Although letter writing is sadly becoming an extinct art (e-mail has revived it slightly), your student can certainly write letters to grandparents, cousins, and close friends.

- *Book writer, illustrator, binder.* These start-to-finish projects don't stop being fun after preschool. Encourage your student to gather his short stories into book form and keep them on the bookshelf.

MOM KNOWS BEST

Because you care enough... Have your child make her own birthday and holiday cards (or cards for "just because").

SPELL SUCCESS

When does spelling become important? In the final draft. Until that point, you want your child to focus on the meat of the story. She can always go back later and correct the spelling, or change a word to make it more expressive.

MOM ALWAYS SAID

Don't get sucked into the "Kids today can't spell" controversy. John F. Kennedy and author F. Scott Fitzgerald were notoriously bad spellers. *The Great Gatsby* reportedly had 5,500 spelling errors in its first draft.

Gud? GD? Good!

Most schools now support the concept of "invented spelling," an approach that encourages kids to spell the word as they hear it. The idea is to focus on meaning rather than spelling. Instead of choosing a simple word that's easy to spell, kids can feel free to go for one that's more interesting or more precise.

As kids read and learn more about the rules of spelling, they develop a richer vocabulary and better spelling skills. When proofreading your child's work, limit your spelling corrections to two at the most. You might point out a misspelled word, if you're sure it was just a careless error and that she knows the correct spelling. You might also point out a commonly used word that's misspelled over and over, so that the mistake doesn't get reinforced. Otherwise, let her teacher handle spelling issues.

Older students, especially those who use a computer for final copy, should proofread their work carefully in addition to running a spell-check. After all, a spell-check won't pick up the misuse of a word, as in the sentence, "Sally went two the store." That kind of mistake needs human eyes to detect.

"Mom, How Do You Spell...?"

Some kids, especially younger students, become fixated on spelling words correctly for their writing projects and are constantly calling out for spelling help while they write. It's better to separate the revision process from the creative one. Encourage your child to get it all down on paper and then go back to correct spelling.

Otherwise, the details of grammar, punctuation, and spelling can interfere with creativity.

Expanding Your Child's Vocabulary

A rich vocabulary is the heart of any piece of writing. Encourage your child to use a thesaurus to enrich her work, and keep one in your home library. Actually, most word processing programs include a thesaurus, putting a better word just a keystroke away.

MOM KNOWS BEST

One teacher listed 90 synonyms for the verb "say" and handed them out at the beginning of the year with the comment: "'Said' is dead—find another word to use." Have your child make up her own list of synonyms for the verb "say."

Games like crossword puzzles, anagrams, and word searches also help expand a kid's vocabulary. Buy books of word puzzles, or make your own.

MOM KNOWS BEST

A great ice breaker at birthday parties is a crossword puzzle with clues about the birthday celebrant. There's software that makes constructing the puzzle a snap.

R-I-T-E? Right!

Invented spelling has no place on a spelling test, however. Some teachers give weekly exams using a spelling or vocabulary book. In the upper grades, some emphasize vocabulary in order to prepare students for college entrance exams.

Check out the spelling test format. Does it include more than just the words on the list? What about words from previous lists? Will the class be asked to write sentences using the spelling words?

Test scores can be frustrating to kids who have completed their assignments and studied their words. Remind your student that you're interested in the process, not the result. Learning how to study effectively is an important lesson in itself.

MOM ALWAYS SAID

Is your student in the top spelling group? A teacher can call the groups bluebirds, robins, and cardinals, but within 30 seconds, the kids know whether they're in the top, average, or low group of any subject. Whichever section your child is in, you want to know:

◆ What was the criteria for assigning students to a group?

◆ Is there any movement among the groups? When and how is that decided?

Surefire Spelling Help

Here are some mom-tested tips for improving spelling test scores:

◆ Encourage your child to make the most of his particular learning style (see Chapter 4). A visual learner might use flash cards, an auditory learner could spell the words into a tape recorder and play them back, a kinesthetic learner could practice the words to a beat, and a tactile learner might benefit from writing them out a few times.

◆ Play a game of Hangman using the spelling words.

◆ Buy software that makes a game out of spelling. *Spellbound* by Davidson is a good one.

◆ Group the words by number of syllables or part of speech (nouns, verbs, adverbs, etc.).

◆ Give your student a pretest on the first day the words are assigned. Then you'll know which words need special attention.

Spelling Drill

1. The student writes each spelling word once.

2. Looking at the list, the student says each word out loud and spells it.

3. The student closes her eyes, Mom says the word, and the child spells it.

4. The student opens her eyes, and Mom administers a written spelling test.

5. The student writes each misspelled word correctly three times.

6. Repeat this drill every night before the test.

GRAMMATICALLY CORRECT

Kids today got no clue about grammar.

It's not quite that bad, but moms do worry that their children wouldn't recognize a run-on sentence if they ran over it. Grandparents lament the absence of grammar drills in today's English classes; in the good old days, they say, the average ninth grader could diagram a sentence in under 30 seconds.

Are drills the answer? Not really, say the experts. In fact, grammar proficiency is more highly correlated to math ability than verbal competence. A child may be able to diagram a sentence and still not be able to construct one on his own.

So what's a mom to do? The best strategy is to encourage your student to read and write. As he reads, he will absorb the techniques of grammar and punctuation that enliven a piece of writing, and as he writes, he will learn to put those techniques into practice.

MOM AS EDITOR

Before you edit your student's writing assignment—as opposed to simply reading it—stop and think. How will your current parent-child relationship weather Mom as Critic? Is that job best left to the teacher? For that matter, how will the teacher feel about parents editing writing projects?

It's not necessarily a sign of a troubled family relationship if comments on a student's writing make him defensive. "Editor" may not be the role he needs you to play. Perhaps you should limit your observations to pointing out a misspelling or two, or a misplaced comma, and leave the rest to the teacher.

Some teachers really want to walk the student through the writing process, from rough draft to finished product. They need to see each stage, warts and all. This may be difficult for some moms to handle, but if you believe your child's teacher is doing a good job, respect his wishes.

What if the teacher doesn't seem to be paying enough attention to the details? Keep the particular writing assignment in mind. Some are intended to familiarize students with a specific technique, such as haiku, a Japanese poetry form. In this case, spelling errors may be less important. Talk it over with the teacher and see whether you can find common ground.

PENMANSHIP IN THE AGE OF COMPUTERS

Doctors have traditionally been excused from legible handwriting. The rest of us, however, have been expected to cultivate a neat and legible script. Has penmanship gone the way of quill pens, now that we have computers? No. Homework may often be done on a computer, but exams are handwritten, and work is still judged, at least in part, by its presentation. The response may be brilliant, but if the teacher can't read the student's answer, it's still going to get a zero.

Give It Time

Boys tend to have more problems with legible handwriting than girls, simply because their fine-motor skills tend to develop a little later. It can be painful to watch a child gripping his pencil tightly as he slowly and laboriously forms the letters. Any interest in writing long and involved stories quickly evaporates under the strain of copying and recopying by hand.

Poor handwriting can signal a learning disability (see Chapter 13), but more often it's simply a question of maturation. Your child's handwriting will improve over time. Because it's a developmental issue, practicing script for hours isn't going to help much, but there are ways you can help. Here are some tips from Carole M. Springer, occupational therapist:

- *Posture.* Poor posture does affect a child's handwriting. Make sure that your student is sitting comfortably and appropriately at a table or desk. No slouching!

- *Cursive.* Most kids find cursive (script) easier than printing because it flows. Students don't have to worry so much about spacing, which some find difficult.

- *Shoulder strength.* Control begins at the shoulder and extends to the fingers. Developing shoulder strength may help your student improve her handwriting. Regular writing practice on a vertical surface like a blackboard, an easel, or a piece of paper taped to the refrigerator will strengthen her shoulder muscles.

- *Pencil grips.* Pencil grips can help modify awkward pencil grasps. They're sold at office supply stores and teacher resource centers.

◆ *The right tool.* "Dr. Grip," by Pilot, provides more control than ordinary pencils. Felt-tip pens are good, too; they flow easily and don't require much pressure.

◆ *Calligraphy.* Some kids find calligraphy more interesting than cursive writing and are more willing to practice it. Calligraphy requires concentration, control, and a very specific way of forming letters. A class or two would help for starting out, but some pens on the market make calligraphy fairly easy, even for beginners.

◆ *Erasable ink.* Erasable pens are a wonderful invention, but they smear more easily, which can compound handwriting problems, especially for lefties.

◆ *Keyboarding.* What can I say? Encourage your student to learn keyboarding as early as possible. She'll use it all her life.

MOM KNOWS BEST

If your child's handwriting is seriously affecting his class-work and test results, consider buying a laptop computer for classroom use and exams. Of course, you'll need to check with the teacher before you do this.

PROOFREADING: THE FINAL FRONTIER

Ah. The creative process is complete. The tome is written. So why is Mom still on her kid's case? Because the project isn't quite finished…yet. Proofreading is a necessary part of any writing project, whether it's a 40-page research paper or a paragraph in response to an exam question.

Proofreading isn't a bad role for you, Mom. Every writer needs help proofing her own work. Writers who are immersed in a project often see what they *intended* better than they see what's actually written on the paper.

Still, your student needs to read her own paper first and make corrections before you get hold of it. Here are basic proofreading tips:

- Read the paper aloud, slowly.

- Cover the rest of the page with a blank piece of paper and focus on one line at a time, so you don't skip ahead or mentally add words that aren't there.

- Read the paper backwards.

THE LEAST YOU NEED TO KNOW

- The more a student reads, the better he writes.

- It works best to separate the writing stage from the editing/proofreading stage. Once your student has gotten her thoughts on paper, then she can go back and clean up spelling and grammar errors.

- Handwriting still counts, but practice may not be the cure for poor penmanship. Your student's fine-motor skills may be lagging, and maturation will help.

- Consider purchasing a laptop computer for your student if poor handwriting is seriously affecting his classwork and test results.

9

It All Adds Up

MOM!!

Lots of kids hate math—lots of moms, too. Math scores in this country continue to be depressing. As John Allan Paulos, mathematics professor at Temple University, points out, "There are differences in math ability just like there are differences in literary ability. But people don't make the comparable arguments saying 'you're not going to be a journalist or novelist, so you might as well as forget the English courses.' They do tend to make that argument when it comes to mathematics."

WHY CARE ABOUT MATH?

There are three good reasons for studying math, even if you're not a "numbers person":

1. As we move into the 21st century, more and more jobs require mathematics. Companies frequently recruit math majors, because analytical skills are invaluable even for non-mathematical jobs.

2. Math literacy makes you a more effective citizen. Unless you're comfortable with numbers and understand what statistics really tell you, the figures bandied about in the media can be misleading. When you have a "feel for numbers," you can accurately interpret your chances of winning the lottery or the relative safety of air travel.

3. Math can be fun! Even more, as philosopher Bertrand Russell observed, the logic, the patterns, the structure of mathematics "possess not only truth, but supreme beauty."

THAT'S WHY YOU HAVE A CALCULATOR

Mathematics is more than arithmetic. Although your kids have to know how to add, subtract, multiply, and divide, that's not the end goal in studying mathematics. That's what a calculator does. "No one gets paid for doing long division anymore," says Dr. Thomas Romberg, professor of curriculum and instruction at the University of Wisconsin, Madison, and director of the National Center for Improving Student Learning and Achievement in Mathematics and Science. "If you've got to do a lot of calculation, it's not done with paper and pencil—except in school." *Mathematics is a way of conceptualizing the world.*

Buy your student a calculator and encourage her to experiment. Eliminating the stress of lengthy calculations allows a child to "play" with numbers. There are books full of calculator games and tricks that grab a child's attention while teaching her how to manipulate numbers.

ATTITUDE COUNTS

You may have to readjust your own anti-math bias first. One of the reasons children in other countries succeed better at math has to do with parental expectations. "It's perfectly all right in the United

States to say 'I wasn't very good at math.' You don't have to be very good," Thomas Romberg points out. "That certainly isn't the case in most European countries or Japan." Parents need to make clear to their children that math literacy is important and possible.

ALL IN THE FAMILY

According to the National Research Council, the performance of the top 5 percent of math students in the United States is matched by the top 50 percent of students in Japan.

MATH IS HANDS-ON

Math shouldn't be a paper-and-pencil subject, at least not entirely. Sure, kids need to memorize math facts and understand math concepts, but they learn math skills better with hands-on activities. Using math manipulatives (tangrams, blocks, and, yes, fingers!) makes math more meaningful and concrete. If your child's school isn't teaching math as a hands-on activity, talk to the teacher and/or principal. (Check the appendix for math education resources.)

TIME'S UP

Separate the issues of understanding math and timed test performance. Lots of kids have trouble with "mad minutes" where you have to complete 30 arithmetic problems in 60 seconds. That doesn't mean they're having trouble with mathematical concepts. The purpose of timed tests is to make basic math facts instinctive— no more counting on fingers to add 9 + 4. Having basic addition, subtraction, and multiplication down cold makes complex subtraction and division problems much easier to solve, but that doesn't take away the feelings of frustration when your student comes up three problems short in a timed test. Remind him that these tests are like practicing scales on a piano: Their purpose is simply to make playing the music of math easier and more enjoyable!

Even a very strong math student may not do well on "mad math" tests. She may:

- Be nervous about tests and quizzes in general

- Need more time to process information

- Need to spend more time memorizing the basics

Often, though, the issue is simply speed: It's hard to perform under pressure, and it's hard to have the answers at your fingertips. Here are some ways you can help:

- *Sympathize with your child's anxiety.* Encourage him to see timed tests as practice in facing pressure situations, not as a judgment on his mathematical prowess.

- *Practice with him at home.* If practice doesn't always make perfect, it does make the process more familiar.

- *Break down the test into parts.* Instead of 30 problems in 60 seconds, try 10 problems in 20 seconds.

MOM KNOWS BEST

Practice math facts without math drills. Have your student add or subtract the numbers on street signs, on license plates, and in the grocery store. Add up (or estimate) the cost of lunch at McDonald's!

LIVING WITH MATH

Look for math opportunities around the house. When cooking, ask your children to measure the ingredients and compare quantities. How much more salt do you use than baking soda? How many cups of flour will we need if we double the recipe? How many people will this dish feed? How about if we halve the recipe? "Math conversations" help kids see that math extends beyond the classroom. Math is part of everyday life and makes life more interesting and understandable.

Here are some more family math activities:

◆ *Savings plus.* Have your student calculate the savings if she buys a coveted pair of jeans on sale or at an outlet center. Take it a step further. If you have to travel a distance to get to the sale, compare the price of gas to the savings. Was it worth it?

◆ *Bottom line.* It's fun for your kid to set up a lemonade stand on the corner, but help make it a real business venture. Have her calculate her expenses (cost of ingredients) and subtract them from her profits.

◆ *Penny-wise.* Start a penny jar for the family. Empty pockets every evening and put pennies in the jar. When the jar is full, use the money for a family treat (ice cream cones for every-one?). Have your student estimate how many pennies are in the jar—then count them.

◆ *Pound-foolish?* Have your student develop a budget for her allowance. Agree that you will give her a raise if she can *prove* she actually needs more money.

◆ *Added dimensions.* When you decorate, get your student involved. Have her measure the walls before you buy wall-paper or paint; then take her to the paint store and have her figure out how much paint or paper you'll need.

◆ *Block building.* Even though your student may be getting older, don't give up those blocks, Legos, or even Lincoln Logs so fast. They're an excellent way to learn about size, shapes (geome-try), and spatial relationships.

In MY Estimation...

Although precise calculation is necessary for many tasks, learning to estimate accurately is equally important. When you estimate, you're actually thinking about the problem, as opposed to applying rote learning. Encourage your student to estimate at home. How much time will it take to complete a certain homework assign-ment? Has she remembered to build in extra time for potential problems? Here are some other estimating games to try:

◆ When driving together, have your child estimate how far it is to your destination, and how long it will take to get there. Check the clock and the odometer when you set out, and again when you get there. How did he do? For extra credit, try computing miles per hour. See whether traffic interferes with his results. Invite your student to develop an alternate route that takes traffic or highway conditions into account.

◆ When shopping in the grocery store, ask your child to estimate the cost of the food in the shopping cart, rounding off to the nearest dollar.

◆ Play estimation games: How many pumpkin seeds in the Halloween pumpkin? How many M&Ms in the bag?

ALL IN THE FAMILY

 In her book *Overcoming Math Anxiety*, Sheila Tobias urges students to continue taking math classes throughout their educational careers: "[Experts] estimate that starting salaries go up $2,000 per year for every mathematics course taken after the ninth grade."

Graphic Illustrations

Graphing teaches relationships among objects and "graphically" illustrates patterns, growth, and decline. Have your kid make graphs of familiar situations—bar graphs, pie charts, and line charts. If you have a computer, go ahead and use it.

Here are some "graph-ic" ideas:

◆ Keep a chart on how much time he spends watching TV, doing homework, playing sports, and reading for fun.

◆ Graph the number and kinds of pets in the neighborhood.

◆ Record the temperature outside each day at a set time. Compare the temperature in front of the house to the temperature in back. Is it different? Why?

◆ Encourage your student to keep her own sports statistics. A Little Leaguer could keep track of her batting average, earned run average, number of bases stolen, and win/loss percentage.

Read the sports pages together and ask your sports fan to explain the charts and graphs to you.

◆ Make a household growth chart, marking each person's height in inches and centimeters on a door or wall. Calculate the percentage of growth from year to year. Did the toddler grow proportionately more than the teenager?

Learn Math, Advance Five Spaces

Okay, board games are fun. They also teach math! If you land on Community Chest, are you more likely on your next roll to land on Park Place or on Boardwalk? Answer: Boardwalk, because there are more possible combinations for rolling a seven with two dice than for rolling a five. Monopoly teaches kids concrete lessons about money when they have to shell out to build houses or pay rent.

Make playing board games a family activity and an opportunity to play with math together. See? It's part of everyday life.

"Are We There Yet, Mom?"

Family car trips are a test of many things! To help ease the strain, here's a way to turn the timeless question of whether we're there yet to educational advantage: Before your next car trip, buy your kids a map and a notebook and help them calculate the distance to your destination, using the map legend as their guide. About how long will it take to cover the distance? Have them write their estimate in the notebook. If the trip will take all day or longer, divide it into stages and get them to write estimates for each stage. Keep track of how close they come with each stage. Maybe they'd like to revise some of their upcoming estimates based on experience.

On a separate page, ask them to keep a record of gas fill-ups and let you know how many miles per gallon your car is getting. Compare highway mileage to city mileage. Is there a difference?

Be creative! How many cows per mile do you see, on average, in a 10-mile stretch of country? Think up your own math games to help the time pass; then turn it around and let your kids design a quiz for you. (How'd you do, Mom?)

MOM ALWAYS SAID

John Allan Paulos says, "Math has as much to do with computation as writing has to do with typing."

Family Math

Does your school hold Family Math Nights? If not, you might want to see if you can get the tradition going. Through a series of workshops, parents and children learn math together. Contact:

> Family Math Program
> The Lawrence Hall of Science
> University of California at Berkeley
> Berkeley, CA 94720-5200
> (510) 642-1823

Ask your librarian or bookseller about interesting math-related books. You may find some books that are just right for your student's age group, including books of puzzles and brain teasers, which many kids find irresistible.

Biographies of mathematicians, business leaders, and scientists may help nurture an older student's math zeal. There are even novels in which math plays a part.

MOM KNOWS BEST

Kids love the *Guiness Book of World Records,* and believe it or not, it's a pretty good educational tool. It makes numbers fun, interesting, and even weird—in a cool way!

"Not Now, Mom, I'm Almost to Level 10!"

Some of the best software is mega-fun and teaches math concepts without being heavy handed. *The Factory* by WINGS is great fun for kids and parents. Available in both English and Spanish, it simulates a factory production line in operation. Players must solve problems involving flaws in production. *Mega Math Blaster,* by

Davidson, has different levels to match increasing math competency. *Algebra Quest,* by Media Quest, finds creative ways to teach math concepts. Kids forget they're playing educational software.

NO CLUE? ASK DR. MATH

So. Your child is having trouble with math homework, and you don't understand it any better than he does. Don't think you're the only person this has ever happened to, Mom. Here's your first line of defense: Ask your student to explain the basic principles involved. Sometimes just going through the steps or reviewing a similar problem helps trigger the answer or suggest strategies.

Swarthmore College offers a lifeline to struggling math students from kindergartners to college seniors! Dial up their Web site, Ask Dr. Math, at *http://forum.swarthmore.edu/dr.math/* and type in your math problem. College students and professors will do their best to help. Pretty cool, huh?

Here are some other great math Web sites that are fun and helpful:

◆ **MegaMath** at **http://www.c3.lanl.gov/mega-math/**

Offers creative and imaginative ideas, exercises, and activities. From the Computer Research and Applications Group at Los Alamos National Laboratory.

◆ **Flash Cards for Kids** at **http://www.wwinfo.com/edu/ flash.html**

This site offers flash card games to reinforce addition, subtraction, multiplication, and division. Goes from the simple to the more complex.

◆ **Math Help** at **http://www.mathleague.com/help/ help.htm**

From the Math League, this site is a resource for students from grades 4 through 8. Gives explanation and examples for topics on whole numbers, decimals, data and statistics, fractions, geometry, and more.

- **MathDEN** at **http://www.actden.com/math-den/**

  Provides "hot math tips" for calculation, math problem sets for grades 7 through 12, and more. You'll need to register (no charge), but you can log in using the id "guest" and the password "guest."

- **Cornell Theory Center Math and Science Gateway** at **http://www.tc.cornell.edu/Edu/mathscigateway/math.html**

  This site offers links todozens of math Web resources for students in grades K through 12. Also includes links for history of mathematics (including biographies of women mathematicians), online math dictionary and math tables, and mathematics software on the Web.

GIRLS AND MATH

Research has shown that girls enjoy math in the early grades but that their interest in math wanes by adolescence. What happens?

- The popular expectation is that boys will do well in math and science and that girls will favor literature and the arts. Eventually this becomes self-fulfilling.

- Toys that stimulate a scientific approach—that encourage building, exploring, and tinkering—are labeled "boys' toys," and many girls don't have the opportunity to play with them.

- Differences in how girls and boys respond to teacher questions contribute to a male-dominated classroom atmosphere. Girls tend to think more before speaking, so they're slower to raise their hands in response to a question. Boys tend to speak as they think and are quicker to respond to a question. Teachers unconsciously reinforce boys' classroom behavior by responding to the child who calls out the answer, rather than the "good" girl who raises her hand. By fifth grade, boys are tending to dominate the classroom, while girls may feel shut out.

- By adolescence, a girl may experience intense peer pressure to avoid appearing "nerdy" or "unfeminine."

MOM ALWAYS SAID

Be careful what you say to your daughter about math. Coming from Mom, a well-meaning "I'm not good at math either" just reinforces the idea that girls aren't good at numbers.

Marie Curie, Sally Ride, and More

Girls need to see women in jobs that use math and science. They don't have to be women in the news. A lot of moms and other women are doctors, building inspectors, and computer store owners. Make sure your daughter meets some of them. Here are some other suggestions:

◆ Encourage your school to celebrate Women's History Month in March.

◆ Have a poster contest for all students that tells the story of a woman they admire and why.

◆ Offer to help the teacher arrange for women with interesting jobs to address the class. You might even work with the school to establish a regular series geared toward meeting women from a variety of professions.

◆ Establish a female mentor program that gives girls the chance to work with women who use science and math in their work.

◆ Suggest a club or lunch hour meeting for girls interested in science and math. This reduces a scientifically inclined girl's sense of isolation.

Stay the Course

Make sure your daughter continues to take math courses every year. In many school systems, you can complete your math (and science) requirements by the end of tenth grade; encourage your daughter to go further, and be there for her if she's tempted to give up.

Math courses tend to track kids at an early age. Check out your school's requirements for high school honors classes before your student begins middle school. In one school system, if a student isn't selected for the "pre-course I" math class in seventh grade, she won't be admitted to "course I" in eighth grade. This, in turn, automatically eliminates her from taking math honors classes in high school. The decision about whether she'll take twelfth-grade calculus is thus effectively made in sixth grade!

MOM ALWAYS SAID

John Allan Paulos says, "Too often women will major in something they're not particularly interested in just to avoid a calculus or statistics requirement. Five years later they're earning one-half as much as the boy who sat next to them who was half as bright—but took math courses."

All-Girl Math

Some co-educational school systems are experimenting with all-girl math classes to make girls feel more comfortable in the classroom setting. Research seems to confirm that girls in these segregated classes achieve higher scores on tests and enjoy math more.

For example, in all-girls schools, 80 percent of students take four years of science and math, compared to a national average of two years for girls in co-educational institutions. Again, in all-girls schools, 48 percent of seniors intend to major in math, science, business, or engineering—double the national average for girls.

Look for activities outside of school that will encourage and promote an interest in math. Check out museum, library, and summer-camp programs where your daughter can enjoy math-related projects. Make sure there's no gender bias in your own home. Assign household tasks equitably.

Do Girls Get "=" Time?

Check out math classes in your child's school to make sure that they offer girls and boys an equal-opportunity education.

◆ Does the teacher treat all students equally?

◆ Does the teacher call on girls as frequently as he or she calls on boys?

◆ Are the math and science expectations of the teacher and counselor the same for girls as for boys?

◆ How many girls are in advanced math classes?

◆ Does the teacher talk down to girls? Does he or she talk to girls about ideas and concepts?

◆ Does the class solve problems, not just practice math facts?

◆ Are there fun activities like a "math team" club, in addition to the regular math curriculum?

◆ Take a look at the math and science textbooks the school uses, especially the illustrations. Do girls seem to be "watchers," and boys "doers," or is it pretty equal? Are there male teachers and female scientists in the illustrations?

THE LEAST YOU NEED TO KNOW

◆ Math is an important subject that both boys and girls need to study.

◆ Math is more than arithmetical calculations. It's a way of critical thinking that applies to many subjects.

◆ Separate timed tests of math facts from understanding math concepts.

◆ Make sure your daughter continues to take math and science courses throughout high school.

◆ Check out math classes in your child's school to be sure that they offer boys and girls an equal-opportunity education.

10

Those Other Subjects

At school today, your child will learn much more than just the three R's. Science, geography, history, and foreign languages may all be part of your child's curriculum. Gym and classes in computers, music, and art are also taught at many middle and high schools. Your child may even have the opportunity to choose some electives.

Both boys and girls take technology and home and career skills. And then there's health and sex ed—no mom wants her child to flunk those! All in all, your child has to juggle a lot academically, and you need to be ready to help.

SCIENTIFICALLY SPEAKING

Your student was born a scientist. Curious about the world around her, she has been studying and discovering what makes things work since birth. Her earliest scientific breakthrough may have been discovering that the pudgy digits at the end of her hand were perfect for sucking!

Whether your child is studying the life cycle of a plant or the transmission of viruses, her science classes should tap into her natural reservoir of curiosity. The objective is to train students to:

◆ Organize their thoughts

◆ Observe carefully

◆ Question the obvious

◆ Predict what *might* happen

◆ Test predictions under controlled conditions

◆ Make sense of the results

You should try to create a home environment that nurtures the scientist in your child. But this doesn't mean buying a Bunsen burner for your basement. Rather, you should seize the scientific opportunities to explore, question, and experiment with your child in daily life. Kids learn best "hands-on." A chore like cooking can be a scientific adventure—even if the result is inedible! And as your kids experiment and discover, they gain confidence in their ability to solve problems.

ALL IN THE FAMILY

 Albert Einstein once remarked, "I think and think for months and years. Ninety-nine times, the conclusion is false. The hundredth time I am right." More than perhaps in any other discipline, in science, kids have to risk failure in order to be effective.

In-School Science

Check out the scientific environment in your child's school by doing the following:

- At Back-to-School Night, ask about the science curriculum: Who teaches science? Are experts brought in to the science class? How often is science taught?

- Is scientific equipment, such as microscopes and magnifiers, available in the classroom?

- Are scientific displays and exhibits presented in the classroom? How about books? Pictures?

- Does the school library have science books? Does the librarian encourage students to read them?

- Are scientific experiments hands-on, or do students watch the teacher demonstrate?

- Is there a collaborative effort among students or do children work alone?

If you believe your school's science curriculum is inadequate:

1. Talk to the principal and, if necessary, the school board. Organize other parents to support the initiative.

2. Volunteer to help in the classroom and/or to chaperon trips to museums and labs.

3. Contact members of the community who might be willing to offer lectures, donate equipment, or act as mentors to science students.

4. Offer to raise funds for science programs and trips.

At-Home Science

You don't need a home lab to encourage science at home. Here are some tips that other moms have found helpful:

- *Collections.* Kids are natural pack rats, and a collection of anything—from string to stamps to rocks—will help your children learn about organizing, cataloguing, and ordering, which are all important scientific concepts.

- *Seize the moment.* Use errand time for science. In the supermarket, talk about how you can tell the difference between ripe and green fruit. At home, take slightly green bananas and put them in a paper bag; why do they ripen? What gas is released in the bag? Watch a sci-fi TV show or movie with your student and then talk about the issues it raised. Observe and record the weather.

◆ *Plant a garden.* Whether you have a window box or a patch of green in the backyard, a garden is a hands-on science experiment accessible to all. Vary the conditions so your student can see how light, water, and fertilizer affect your growing plants. Are there natural repellents to keep bugs off the plants and other animals from eating them?

◆ *Read books and articles on science.* There's a wealth of science books for kids; ask your librarian for suggestions. Talk about articles in newspapers and magazines that feature scientific issues. Read biographies of scientists.

MOM KNOWS BEST

The Consumer Information Center (CIC) publishes "Books for Children," an annual listing of the best books recently published for preschool through junior high school–age children. It includes books on science and nature. Available from the CIC, Pueblo, CO 81009, for $1.

You can also check out *Odyssey*, a science magazine for elementary and middle school students. The magazine is published nine times a year, costs $26.95, and is available from Cobblestone Publishing, (800) 821-0115.

◆ *Visit museums.* Many cities have natural history museums and hands-on science centers, which are kid magnets. Don't feel like you have to see everything in one trip. Visit often, and concentrate on one or two exhibits each time you go. Allow time for discussion and questions.

◆ *Surf the Net.* The Internet has a wealth of scientific sites that are fun and interesting. Two good ones are: The American

Association for the Advancement of Science (http://www.aaas.org) and The National Science Teachers Association (http://www.nsta.org). NASA has a site at http://www.nasa.gov.

Girls and Science

The number of girls in advanced science classes is small (just like mathematics—see Chapter 9). The issues are similar. The American Association for the Advancement of Science has several publications and a video that may help.

- *Girls and Science* is a quarterly newsletter that focuses on activities, resources, and opportunities in science and mathematics for girls and the adults who work with them. It can be ordered via the Association's Web site (see above) and costs $6.

- *In Touch with Girls and Science,* edited by Margaret E. Tunstall and Marsha Lakes Matyas (1995), provides hands-on activities designed to spark girls' interest in science and mathematics. It includes mentoring tips, suggestions for motivating girls, references, and a resource list. It is available at the Web site (see above) and costs $19.95.

- *Girls, Science and Mathematics* is a 17-minute video for classroom teachers and adult leaders who work with girls. It includes ways to promote girls' interest in science and mathematics and addresses gender equity issues. Available through the Web site, it costs $15.

MOM KNOWS BEST

Consider a science or history theme for your child's next birthday party. Invite the guests to come as individuals from history—dressed in period costume and with a series of clues about who they are. Or host an Invention Convention, inviting guests to design and/or build machines to solve daily problems. The inventions can be wacky or realistic—in either case, kids are developing critical thinking skills.

SOCIAL STUDIES FOR SOCIAL KIDS

You need to help your kids put history and geography in perspective. History is more than a study of dead presidents and world wars. Geography is more than a bunch of maps. But unfortunately, that's what history and social studies classrooms often become. You must make history and geography come alive for your children to be successful social studies students.

Don't Know Much About History (and Geography)

Remember your high school history class, when the teacher had to cover everything from the beginning of time to the present day in one school year? And geography lessons that were all about finding the longitude and latitude of exotic places, but nothing about who lived there? How have things improved? You can find out by asking your child's teacher about the curriculum.

Here are some questions to ask about the history curriculum:

◆ Does the teacher anticipate covering all the required material in class? If not, are students responsible for learning the additional material on their own?

◆ Is the class primarily taught in lecture format?

◆ What is the reading material? Will the students study any original sources? Will the students do any independent historical research?

◆ How are current events integrated into the curriculum?

◆ Are there state competency tests? How are students prepared for these tests?

◆ How are course grades determined? Are tests multiple-choice, essay, or a combination? If the tests are primarily multiple-choice, then the course emphasis is on facts and dates, rather than on the interpretation and analysis of events. Your student needs both.

MOM ALWAYS SAID

If your student is not a strong reader and is having difficulties with the class text, ask about alternatives. Teachers can often provide easier textbooks that cover the same material.

Here are some questions to ask about the geography curriculum:

◆ Is a study of different cultures integrated into the curriculum?

◆ Are maps and materials up to date? With the changing face of the world, maps that are as little as a year old may be out of date.

◆ Does the class study how native cultures have evolved and adapted in response to changing physical conditions?

◆ Do teachers include sensitivity training and units on tolerance as part of the study of different cultures?

Homemade History

History is the story of people and events and a record of the past. By definition, your child's birth is a historical event, and she needs to know it. Making your student realize that *she* is part of history may make her more curious about the subject. Here are nine ways you can make history come alive. Some are great for class history projects or extra credit.

◆ *Make a family tree.* This is a project the whole family can enjoy. Four great books can help: *Do People Grow on Family Trees?: Genealogy for Kids and Other Beginners: The Official Ellis Island Handbook* by Ira Wolfman (Workman Publishers, 1991); *The Complete Idiot's Guide to Genealogy* by Christine Rose and Kay Germdin Ingalls (Macmillan Gereral Reference, 1997); *The Great Ancestor Hunt: The Fun of Finding Out Who You Are* by Lila Perl (Houghton Mifflin, 1989); and *Where Did You Get Those Eyes?* by Kay Cooper (Walker and Company, 1988).

◆ *Volunteer with your child at your local (or county) historical society.* Most societies can use all the help they can get. Some of the work is painstaking (and occasionally boring), but you and your child will learn about documentation, cataloguing, and preservation. (This kind of volunteer work looks great on a college application.)

◆ *Develop an oral and/or video history project.* Whether it's videotaping or talking to elderly members of your family or the senior citizens in your community, this is a great way for students to combine the technology of today with the events of the past. Learn about history and preserve it.

◆ *Read or watch historical fiction and nonfiction.* The books of Laura Ingalls Wilder (*Little House on the Prairie* books) and Jane Austen (*Emma, Sense and Sensibility, Pride and Prejudice*), among others, teach about specific historical periods. *The Diary of Anne Frank* will give your child an insight into the horrors of the Holocaust in a way that no history textbook could ever do. The American Girls collection of books and dolls (The Pleasant Company), which depicts girls in six different periods in American history, helps modern kids relate to long ago times and places.

◆ *Read newspapers and magazines, scan online news reports, and join in online discussions about what's happening.* Discuss current events at the dinner table. Model good citizenship by voting.

◆ *Volunteer with your child in a political campaign.* Grassroots politics is a perfect introduction to the political process. Whether it's stuffing envelopes, handing out campaign literature, staffing rallies, or manning telephones, your child will learn about how politics works. Check out *The War Room*, a documentary on the Clinton 1992 Presidential campaign—it's funny and insightful.

◆ *Play period games and cook using historical recipes.* Ever rolled a hoop? Baked bread (sans a bread machine)? Activities like these will help your children better understand what their historical counterparts did years ago.

◆ *Visit historical preservation sites or local reenactments.* Colonial Williamsburg is a great family vacation (with access to modern amusement parks as well). Smaller working farms and historical sites can also give your children an insight into ways of life that no longer exist.

◆ *Surf the Net.* Check out the Cobblestone Publishing home page (http://www.cobblestone.com). This firm publishes three history magazines: *Calliope: World History for Young People* (for grades 6 through 8); *Cobblestone: The History Magazine for Young People* (for grades 4 through 8); and *FACES*, an introduction to diverse cultures throughout the world. Each magazine is published nine times per year, and a subscription costs $26.95. All three magazines have age-appropriate activities, and *Calliope* and *Cobblestone* both sponsor fun contests. Call (800) 821-0115 to order.

◆ *There's fun and an educational experience in new software,* like *Oregon Trail II* by MECC, a history simulation game that lets the players assume the roles of westward emigrants of the 1840s and '50s. The company has similar products for reliving the history and geography of other regions, such as *The Yukon Trail, The Amazon Trail,* and *MayaQuest.* For more information, call (800) 215-0368.

Home-Grown Geography

Geography is easy to integrate into your family life. The following ideas might not make your child ready for a Mount Everest expedition, but she'll at least be eager to read about one.

◆ *Subscribe to* National Geographic *and its kids' publication,* World. It offers your child a glimpse into cultures and animals in far-away places. Check out the *National Geographic* Web site: http://www.nationalgeographic.com. (If *National Geographic* is too difficult for your student to read by herself, read stories of interest together.)

◆ *Incorporate geography lessons into family meals.* If your student is studying China, order in Chinese food (or make your own). You can find many specialty foods at most large supermarkets or via mail order.

◆ *Appoint your child the family navigator.* Have her map out a route when you go on vacation or just run errands in town.

◆ *Have your child create a map of the mall.* Ask her to point out the path to her favorite stores.

◆ *Encourage your child's school administrators to have the school participate in the National Geographic Geography Bee or the Geography Olympiads.*

◆ *Ask your child to map out her favorite sports teams.* Take a map of the United States. Locate and mark the towns of her favorite teams. Ask your child to find out *how* the teams got their names (for example, why is the football team from Pittsburgh called the Steelers?).

◆ *Buy a compass.* Just playing with the compass in your home (which way does her room face?) will teach your child about direction.

◆ *To make distance a more concrete concept for your child, walk a mile with her.* Let her see how long it takes. Time a mile while driving in the car. Then have her determine how long it will take to travel to the family vacation destination.

PARLEZ VOUS FRANÇAIS? HABLA ESPAÑOL?

At some point in your child's academic career, she will have the opportunity to study a foreign language. Besides learning how to order in a restaurant, what does a student learn from studying a foreign language? All the following:

◆ A deeper understanding of different countries, customs, cultures, and history.

◆ A sensitivity and awareness of the English language.

◆ Greater communication and connections with foreign language speakers at home and abroad.

On a very practical level, most colleges expect students to have taken a minimum of two years of a foreign language. Furthermore, foreign language fluency is a significant asset when job hunting.

Choosing a Language

Your student's language choice will probably be based on availabiity and interest. Generally, some of the Romance languages (French, Spanish, and sometimes Italian) are the most commonly offered courses. However, more and more schools are now offering other languages, such as Chinese and Russian.

Latin has unfortunately become more of a rarity. One mom regretfully points out, "I learned more about grammar by taking Latin than I ever learned in English class."

How to choose? Your student may want to study a Romance language because Spanish, French, and English share a common foundation. For that reason, the vocabularies of these languages may be easier to learn (although the grammar rules for each is different). You may also want your child to take up French or Spanish because you studied one of these languages yourself and believe it will be simpler to help with a familiar subject. Finally, there's the very practical approach of one mom who encouraged her seventh grader to take Spanish because the French teacher was reputed to be so bad!

However, job forecasters suggest that fluency in Chinese and Russian will be important in the 21st century. If your child chooses to study one of these languages, keep in mind:

◆ He will have to learn a new alphabet (and style of printing).

◆ Fluency is much more difficult to attain.

◆ Most school systems have a single teacher for these languages. This means that if your student begins studying either language, he will have the same teacher throughout high school. If the teacher-student chemistry is good, terrific. If not, you don't have the recourse of asking for a different teacher.

Learning the Language

You don't have to be fluent in a language to help your child succeed at it. The most important ingredient in language achievement is *staying on top of assignments*. Learning any language is a building process; each new lesson is predicated on the previous one. Here's how you can help your child:

◆ *Make sure that she completes each homework assignment and reviews and understands each day's lesson* (even if there's no specific homework that night).

◆ *Have her maintain a vocabulary list of new words she's learning.* This will be helpful for test review and for essay work.

◆ *Incorporate what she's learning into your household routine.* Prepare native foods. If you have cable TV, seek out programs that are broadcast in the language she's studying. (One seventh-grade Spanish student, also a soccer fan, watched the Spanish-language station to catch weekly overseas soccer games.)

◆ *Surf the Net.* Check out the official home pages of France, Spain, China, etc. Foreign magazines, tourist attractions, and museums all have Web sites. At Les Premiers Pas sur l'Internet, for example, your student will find material created by and for French children, including games, stories, reviews, and jokes.

EXTRA ELECTIVES

Besides the academic subjects, your student will also have to take a variety of other classes. These may include music, art, computer skills, keyboarding, technology, home and career skills, gym, and sex education. These extras enrich your student's education, but also put more demands on her time.

One of these "extras" may turn out to be your student's favorite subject—and teach her more than you might expect. One mom discovered that her son, a lackluster student, adored his gourmet cooking class. He had never shown any previous interest in meal preparation, but he was suddenly coming home with exotic recipes that he was eager to prepare. Beyond the great meals that his family began to enjoy, he learned about organization and attention to detail—skills that are necessary to be both a good cook and a good student.

Some points to remember about special classes:

◆ *Make sure your student provides you with a list of the materials and supplies she needs for the class at the beginning of the term.* For example, in home and career skills, your student may have a sewing project that requires fabric. You don't want to be told at 8 P.M. as the mall is closing that she needs it for class the next morning. Part of your student's grade may depend upon meeting deadlines (including bringing in materials on the assigned day).

◆ *At Back-to-School Night, ask how the teacher will determine grades.* What percentage of the grade is based on the process, and how much is determined by the finished product? Your child's grade in art, for example, should not be based on whether her drawings are museum quality. Rather, the question is whether she followed directions, learned techniques, brought an energy and enthusiasm to the class, and completed her assignments on time.

◆ *Insist that your student be attentive to electives' requirements.* Even if she thinks these classes are silly, she needs to respect the teachers and meet the requirements. Remember, grades from these classes appear on your student's transcript and can affect her average. One mom discovered that her straight-A student didn't make the honor roll because of a C he received in his photography class. The student frequently fooled around during class, ignored deadlines, and didn't complete all his assignments. That kind of attitude gets a student a bad reputation.

◆ *Watch that your student keeps things in balance.* On the other hand, while it's terrific if your student is enthusiastic about one of her electives, don't let her performance in core subjects suffer.

THE LEAST YOU NEED TO KNOW

- ◆ Incorporate subjects like geography and science into your home life. Make history come alive by making your student realize she's part of history.

- ◆ Success in a foreign language class requires that your student stay on top of all her assignments.

- ◆ At Back-to-School Night, be sure you understand the requirements of all your student's classes, including the electives. Get the list of required supplies early in the term.

- ◆ Make sure your child treats elective courses as seriously as core courses.

Academics Is More Than Books

The goal of education is not just to develop a good student, but to produce a well-rounded individual who's interested in books and much more. Your child will learn as much on the ball fields, in the orchestra pits, and at comic book conventions (!), as she will in the classroom. The old adage, "All work and no play makes Jack a dull boy" has never been truer. You want your student to be multi-faceted, to develop all sides of her personality.

ON THE BALL FIELDS OF LIFE

Twenty million kids participate in organized sports. Sports offer our kids a fun way to get physically fit—and much more. Consider the "academic" skills students need to exercise in order to succeed at sports:

- ◆ A student needs to understand the *math* involved in angle shots, vectors, and statistics.

- ◆ A student needs to know *science* to appreciate wind resistance, ball trajectories, gravity, and the effects of nutrition and exercise.

- ◆ A student needs to appreciate the *history* of the game to understand which strategies have worked in the past and which haven't.

- ◆ A student must take the *geography* and topography of the playing field into account when planning game strategy.

Organized sports build not only a student's muscles, but her mind as well.

Sports Teach Much More

Beyond the "academics," students who play organized sports also learn:

- ◆ The rewards of hard work and practice.

- ◆ The meaning of teamwork; getting along with peers and coaches.

- ◆ How to put winning and losing into perspective.

- ◆ Problem-solving skills (figuring out game-winning strategies; learning to juggle competing demands).

- ◆ Commitment to an interest.

Of course, the key is whether the adults (coaches and parents) have the right attitude about sports, model good behavior, and supervise student athletes carefully. Under the right circumstances, a good coach, like a gifted teacher, can have an incredible influence on your child and can affect her performance both on the field and in the classroom.

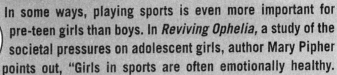

MOM KNOWS BEST

In some ways, playing sports is even more important for pre-teen girls than boys. In *Reviving Ophelia,* a study of the societal pressures on adolescent girls, author Mary Pipher points out, "Girls in sports are often emotionally healthy. They see their bodies as functional not decorative. They have developed discipline in the pursuit of excellence. They have learned to win and lose, to cooperate, to handle stress and pressure. They are in a peer group that defines itself by athletic ability rather than popularity, drugs or alcohol use, wealth or appearance."

Are Sports Only for the Athletically Gifted?

Participating in organized sports is good for the athlete and nonathlete alike. Consider:

◆ If your child is not a strong student, athletics may be an arena in which she can excel and be a leader. Her participation in sports may also inspire her to achieve academically, since most schools mandate a certain level of academic achievement for athletes to remain on the team. (If not, you should set your own academic standards for your child.)

◆ If your child is a strong student, but not a particularly good athlete, sports offer her the opportunity to meet and value kids unlike herself. Sports are also a way she can challenge herself, a place where success is not automatic.

Participating in organized sports can build your child's self-esteem, even if she's not the star fielder. Again, with the right coach and the proper mom-attitude, your student-athlete will learn that competing is not solely a question of winning or losing, but a quest for self-improvement.

ALL IN THE FAMILY

Some kids hope that sports will be their ticket to success. But one study showed that only 25 percent of youth baseball stars went on to be stars on their high school varsity teams. Remind your student that education is the best means to lifetime success.

Setting Priorities

It's easy to say that academics must always be your child's first priority, but what do you do when your child is in the middle of soccer playoffs *and* has a book report due the next day? In the midst of hockey season, do you let your student settle for a B on a science project, when you know that with a little more effort and time, his grade might have been a B+ or even an A?

For your child's sake, the basic rule has got to remain: *school comes first*. That said, it's up to you and your child to determine how to budget his study time so that schoolwork doesn't suffer when sports demands are especially heavy.

Here are some tips:

♦ *Plan ahead.* This is the most important lesson your student can learn. He's got to look at the big picture: What are his assignments? When are his games? Then he has to figure out when he has time to do his assignments, working ahead on game-free days.

♦ *Use time wisely.* Your child needs to learn how to use snippets of time. During travel time to and from games or practices, for example, your student can read or even listen to books on tape. While waiting for the coach or the game to begin, have a book in your child's team bag.

♦ *Talk to teachers.* If your student is going to miss classes, he needs to talk to his teachers *ahead of time* and arrange to make up the work. You want teachers to know that your student understands that school comes first and that his work will not suffer because of his involvement in sports.

◆ *Can you help?* There's a difference between doing the assignment and helping your child succeed. You can help by showing him *how* to get organized and working with him to develop a reasonable study schedule. You can do some of the legwork, as long as it's clear who's in charge of the project. For example, if he gives you a list of books he needs from the library, you could pick them up.

◆ *Play to your athlete's strengths.* If your child has the opportunity to choose a writing, reading, or science project, suggest that he incorporate his interest in sports. The book report could be on an athlete he admires; the science project might study how changes in tennis balls affect velocity; the math project could analyze sports statistics. It's easier for a student to work on a project that captures his interest.

MOM KNOWS BEST

Remind your child of the organizational skills listed in Chapter 3 when she's trying to juggle academic responsibilities with team demands:

◆ Do the most difficult homework assignment first.

◆ Do what's required first; save the extra credit for extra time.

◆ The day before a test, study exam material first.

WINNING AND LOSING

Developmentally, it's typical for children to see things in black and white. Games and grades are often reduced to win-loss columns. But with that kind of reasoning, a kid's self-esteem is in peril, dependent on conditions (like ref calls, coaching, and luck) that she can't control. You need to help your child put both games *and* grades into a win-win perspective.

Success is not whether your child's batting average is better than her teammate's, or even if the team wins or loses. Instead, help her focus on realistic goals for personal improvement, such as improving her time by just one second in the 400 meter run. She needs to learn that she won't hit a grand slam each time she's at bat, nor will her team necessarily have an undefeated season. But by removing the emphasis from winning or losing, your child can enjoy and learn from sports.

Cut from the Team

Recreation athletic leagues are terrific because they generally offer a place for all children, no matter what their athletic ability. In the earlier grades, these leagues generally allow each child a minimum amount of playing time.

But as your student athlete gets older, the teams may become more select, so that only the more athletically gifted children may be invited to play. (Even if there's a no-cut policy, your child may spend an inordinate amount of time on the bench.) Or your child may simply age out of the recreation league.

Being cut from the team, or not being selected for the all-stars, can be a devastating blow to a child's ego. If your child is cut, you'll need to help him channel his energies in different directions.

ALL IN THE FAMILY

 One 14-year-old was despondent when he didn't make the ninth-grade basketball team. His mom begged him to go out for the school fencing team, which had a no-cut policy. Just to get his mom off his back, he agreed to try it once and only once. But once was enough...he got hooked on fencing and went on to place in the Nationals!

Here are some tips that may help him through this tough time:

◆ *Acknowledge your child's disappointment.* Don't try to minimize the hurt your child feels. Nor is this the time to point out that your child is gifted in other areas. One straight-A student confessed she would have traded any one of her good grades for a shining moment on the soccer field.

◆ *Suggest that your child try a new sport.* Often the track team and swim team have no-cut policies. These are great sports, especially for less athletic children, because they primarily emphasize improving personal time rather than winning competitions. Or encourage your child to try non-organized sports, such as yoga or aerobics, to stay in shape without the stress and competition of organized sports.

I Quit?!?

At some point, your student may announce that he wants to quit the team. Help him put the issue in perspective. The most important question to ask is: Why?

Perhaps his interests have changed. He wants to give up soccer so he can concentrate on tennis, or he no longer enjoys baseball and doesn't want to spend his Saturdays on the ball field. Okay, that's reasonable. Let your kids sample different activities until they find ones they enjoy and in which they excel. (Of course, giving up competitive sports doesn't mean becoming a couch potato. Suggest that your student find other ways to keep physically fit.)

It's reasonable to insist that your student remain on the team until the end of the season. Since one of the important lessons of playing a sport is learning about teamwork and reliability, your student owes it to his teammates to finish out the season—and play his best.

But what if the decision is *not* based on your child's lack of interest, but is rather a result of poor coaching, repeated criticism about performance, or too much stress?

Sports are supposed to build a child's self-esteem, not destroy it. If your kid is reacting to the behavior of the coaches or the adults who stand on the sidelines, then it's time to step in and help. Speak to the coach who is hyper-critical; insist on (and model) good sidelines behavior from the spectators; help your student put his performance in perspective.

Sports are supposed to be fun. Don't let the grown-ups take the fun out of sports for your child.

JOIN IN

Your child doesn't have to be on a sports team to learn the value of cooperation, hard work, and responsibility. Whether she plays in the school band, participates in student government, or writes for the school newspaper, she learns how to be part of a larger community. And, of course, her volunteer efforts don't have to be school-related. A church/synagogue youth group, a local community organization, Boy/Girl Scouts, and 4-H, for example, are all wonderful opportunities for your student to be part of a group effort.

On a practical level, colleges are looking for students who contribute to their communities (at the school, local, and even state and national level). They want kids who make a difference. It's better for your child to be an active member of two or three clubs than to have an application full of empty memberships.

College recruiters will want to know how involved your student has become in extra-curriculars: How long has she been a member of the club? What leadership positions has she held?

For example, one student who loved to play soccer highlighted his sports-related experiences on his college applications:

◆ Varsity player for his high school team

◆ Player on a select team outside of school

◆ Sports editor of the high school newspaper

◆ U.S. certified soccer referee

The colleges this student applied to were impressed by his ability to approach his interest in soccer from several different angles.

Contributing to his school and community through volunteer work is good for your student and gives him an important education not found in a classroom.

MUSIC HATH CHARMS

Learning to play a musical instrument is another way to enrich your student's intellectual life. Besides the joy of making music, learning music teaches academic skills as well. For example, fractions become concrete when the musician understands the difference between a half and a quarter note. Plus, taking music lessons instills a sense of discipline and commitment.

But many kids lose interest in music when the initial excitement is replaced by the drudgery of practice. In this case, remind your student that practice makes perfect.

Although your child may pressure you to let her quit, don't be too quick to agree. Sometimes, with just a little patience and time, she will get proficient enough to make music fun again.

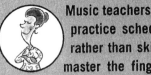

MOM KNOWS BEST

Music teachers advise that your child follow a regular daily practice schedule—even if it's just 15 minutes a day—rather than skip days. By practicing daily, your child will master the fingering easier and will also learn to make music a part of his daily life.

On the other hand, you need to know when to end the battle over the instrument. One mom finally gave up when she discovered her son laying on his back on his bed, holding his cello to his chest, as he mechanically went through the motions of practicing. This was a student who excelled in many other areas, and music was his parents' dream, not his. As with much of parenting, it's a question of picking your battles; if you find that there are other, more important issues, then it's time to put an end to the war over music.

PACK RAT OR COLLECTOR?

Collecting something—whether baseball cards, rocks, stamps, stickers, dolls and doll house furniture, or even comic books—teaches your student about organization, patterns, categorization, and value. It gives your student a focus and broadens his interests.

Collecting is also a wonderful way to relieve the stress of life. Kids often don't feel like they're in control of very much. But they *can* be in charge of their collections. Equally important, when your student becomes a collector, he becomes an expert at something—an important factor at a time in his life when adults seem to be "experts" at most everything. Although he may not know everything there is to know about stamps, rocks, or stickers, he undoubtedly is the master of his holdings, able to recount every last one in his collection.

Collecting also teaches children about trading and bartering, and it provides a way to socialize with other kids.

ALL IN THE FAMILY

Three eighth-grade boys turned their interest in comic books into a viable business. They culled their collections, invested some of their own money to buy comics they believed would increase in value, and then printed and distributed a catalogue of comics for sale. Besides the fun that these kids had, think of the academic skills they needed to use in order to make their business profitable!

Putting On the Brakes

Before your child spends his entire allowance on his collection, you need to set some ground rules:

◆ *As always, school comes first.* If collecting is bordering on an obsession and interfering with academics, you need to apply the brakes and refocus his attention.

◆ *Set a limit on how much of your child's own money he can spend on his collection.* Learning to budget is part of the educational value of collecting.

◆ *Encourage your student to research his interest.* Have him take out books from the library on the subject.

◆ *Help him catalogue his collection.* Show him how to make an index card for each new addition, marking the date bought and the amount spent.

The long-term monetary value of your child's collection is less important than helping him develop a focus and interest. While some collections may retain and perhaps increase in value (for example, stamps, coins, and baseball cards), others (like troll dolls) may never recover their monetary value.

Surf the Net

The Internet is a great place to research a collection and find other collectors. Show your child how to use a search engine, like Yahoo!, to locate Web sites. But kids need to understand some basic ground rules for safety on the Internet:

◆ Never give out your user password to anyone. (No legitimate online service representative will ever ask for it.)

◆ If you permit your child to go online without adult supervision, remind him not to give out his full name, address, or home phone number. Should he want to trade or buy something from another collector online, an adult should supervise the transaction.

HANDS UP: VOLUNTEER WORK

Kids learn a lot from volunteer work. Encouraging your child to do some form of service teaches her lessons she won't find in the classroom, but which will directly impact her educational experience—and her life. Increasingly, school districts are requiring students to perform community service as a graduation prerequisite.

But you don't have to wait until high school for your student to volunteer. Elementary and middle school students can:

◆ Read to younger students.

◆ Clear sidewalks, rake leaves, and mow lawns for neighborhood senior citizens.

◆ Run errands for the housebound.

◆ Bake or prepare treats or simple meals (with adult supervision) for those in need.

◆ Help (with adult supervision) at a soup kitchen or food pantry.

◆ Baby-sit or entertain the children of adult volunteers.

◆ Tutor.

Your local community center and religious organizations are good places to find volunteer jobs.

GET A JOB

In your student's busy schedule, is there time for a paying job? Maybe, yes. Paying jobs can be great learning experiences, give your student a little financial independence, and teach old-fashioned standards of dependability and reliability.

How old should your student be before she gets a job? By the time your student is in seventh grade, she can begin looking for a traditional first job: baby-sitter/mother's helper, snow shoveler, lawn care provider, pet sitter, or golf caddie.

MOM KNOWS BEST

Encourage your child to be creative in finding and landing jobs. One seventh grader used the graphics program on his home computer to develop a flyer advertising his lawn care service. He distributed the flyer throughout the neighborhood and lined up enough jobs to fill five summer mornings.

Another enterprising high schooler took the desktop publishing skills he learned from working on his school newspaper and parlayed them into a freelance job creating newsletters for local businesses. His hourly pay? $20.

How Much Is Too Much?

Keep a careful eye on how much your student works. Researchers at Stanford and Temple Universities found that students who work more than 20 hours a week are more likely:

♦ To have lower grades than their nonworking peers, since they have less time to devote to their studies.

♦ To be more detached from their parents, since they have less time to devote to family activities.

♦ To have a higher rate of alcohol and drug use, since they have more discretionary income.

If your child decides to try a part-time job, remind him that his full-time job is school. Make sure that he:

♦ Does not cut corners academically in order to work.

♦ Does not take fewer challenging courses in order to relieve academic pressures.

♦ Does not sacrifice other extra-curricular activities. While the job is terrific, it should not be his sole outside activity.

You can set limits on how much your student works. Some moms say no to any baby-sitting on school nights; others let their children work up till 9 P.M., presuming all homework is done. Decide what you think your student is capable of doing without impairing her schoolwork, and don't hesitate to revisit the issue if you see that academic problems are beginning to surface.

Work Rules for Kids

If your student is 14 and wants to get an official part-time job, she may need to get a work permit (required in most states). Usually, you can get working papers from the school guidance office. To apply, she'll need to get your permission (usually on a standard form), as well as proof of age.

Federal child labor laws limit the number of hours a 14 or 15-year-old can work:

◆ No more than three hours on a school day or 18 hours in a school week.

◆ No more than eight hours on a non-school day or 40 hours in a non-school week.

◆ Not before 7 A.M. or after 7 P.M., except during the summer when they can work until 9 P.M.

SUMMER PLANS: MORE SCHOOL? WHAT ELSE?

Summertime should be easy. Summer vacation is an opportunity for your student to rest up from the pressures of schoolwork and recharge. It's a chance to try something different. Your student may be interested in camp, volunteer work, a job, or maybe just hanging out with friends.

But although school is closed, that doesn't mean your child shouldn't crack a book over the next 10 weeks. Encourage your student to continue to read during summer vacation. Many schools have a required reading list for the summer. If not, develop your own requirements.

Many public school systems, private schools, and colleges offer summer programs for enrichment or acceleration. (Some also offer classes for remediation; see Chapter 12.) Sometimes these courses offer an opportunity to explore a topic in more detail. For example, writing seminars give students a chance to focus on style and creativity, something often not possible in the rush of the regular school year.

Or your student may be interested in accelerating a specific subject. One student enrolled in an advanced math class over the summer in order to be able to enter the honors math program in the fall. Another student began taking summer classes in order to accumulate enough credits to graduate from high school a year early.

Before you sign your child up for an academic class in the summer, consider:

◆ *If your student accelerates his studies during the summer, will there be appropriate classes for him to take throughout his school career?* For example, if he takes an advanced placement science class in the summer, will there be interesting science courses for him to take during the school year?

◆ *Will he grow and mature more by doing something different during the summer?* For some academically strong students, it might be more important to challenge them in nonacademic ways.

Your local high school, community college, and library may have catalogues and brochures of summer opportunities for students.

THE LEAST YOU NEED TO KNOW

◆ By playing organized sports, your child can reinforce his academic skills and also learn important life skills.

◆ Encourage your student to join a club, sport, or service activity.

◆ Working can teach your child important lessons about responsibility and finance. If your child chooses to work, make sure his academics don't suffer.

◆ Summer is a good time for your child to explore nonacademic subjects. If she opts to take academic classes, be sure that you consider the long-term effect of acceleration.

12

Turned Off and Tuned Out

Most children enter kindergarten full of promise and excited about learning. But within a few years, "I hate school" becomes a common kid complaint. For most kids, declaring that "School stinks" is almost a rite of childhood. It's what's "expected" of kids. The most popular young characters on TV are always plotting how they can skip school (and of course are invariably caught by their wise moms). But some kids really are turned off by school; unless you step in, precious years of learning will be lost.

"I HATE SCHOOL!"

You may have been expecting your student to declare his disgust with school for months. Or you may be surprised when one morning your child refuses to get dressed and finally confesses, "I hate school." Or your child may indicate with other words and actions that he's unhappy with school. It's time to play detective and figure out what's going on.

Just like us moms, kids can have a bad day. Your child may yell "School stinks!" on a day when he does poorly on a test, or gets pushed in the halls, or is yelled at unfairly by a teacher. Or maybe it rained and he had to sit in the auditorium during lunch recess and watch a stupid video.

Sometimes, your child may hate school simply because it's a beautiful day and he would rather be outside playing than sitting in a classroom. Or maybe it's crummy outside, and he would rather stay at home snuggled under a comforter watching TV. Who hasn't had feelings like this?

You need to determine if your child's dislike of school is a temporary phase or a symptom of something more serious. Allow your student to talk about his discontent. Probe to discover the root of the unhappiness. Then, try to help your child come up with a solution. For example, can your student go to the library instead of the auditorium during rainy days?

If you suspect that your child's disenchantment with school stems from more serious problems, read on.

GIRLS AT RISK

In *Reviving Ophelia,* author Mary Pipher warns that the cliques and social pressures of early adolescence transform many previously academically strong girls into school-hating, underperforming students.

Once your daughter enters early adolescence, you'll need to be especially vigilant of what's going on in not only the classrooms, but also in the school halls. How is your daughter faring with her peers? Do her friends value school or make fun of successful students, calling them "nerds"? Does your child have friends to eat with at lunch? Is she harassed by other students?

You may still think of her as your baby, but chances are your daughter is confronting issues about sex, alcohol, and drugs as she's entering adolescence. She may declare that she hates school because school has become an intolerable place to be.

More than ever, parents need to listen carefully to what their daughters are—and aren't—saying about school. If you discover that the social situation at your daughter's school is unbearable, that other students are harassing her or making her life miserable, call the school counselor and principal. This is not a problem your daughter can solve on her own. More than ever, she needs the love and support of her family, even when she's telling you to "Leave me alone."

MENTAL HEALTH DAYS

Sometimes kids will act as if they have been struck down by the bubonic plague when all they have is a simple cold. Moaning, groaning, and begging you to allow them to stay home, their symptoms disappear by 10 o'clock in the morning, just as the first game shows begin on TV.

In this case, you need to trust your instincts. If your student doesn't abuse your trust, he should be allowed the indulgence of an occasional day off (even if he's exaggerating his symptoms). If your hard-working, responsible student asks for a day to recover and recoup once in a while, consider granting him a mental health day. (Of course, this means that your student isn't taking the day off because he doesn't want to take a test or because he hasn't completed an assignment. Furthermore, he has to be prepared to make up any work that he misses.)

What you really want to do is help your child develop a sense of judgment and responsibility. He needs to learn that there will be times in life when he has to hold himself together—even if he does feel sick—and complete an assignment or meet a deadline, just like grown-ups do. If he can develop that kind of judgment and self-motivation, then he will not only be a good student, but he'll be on his way to becoming a responsible adult as well.

MOM ALWAYS SAID

Most school systems commonly permit 15 days per year for excused absences. But if your child actually does miss that much school, he's missing 8.3 percent of his formal classroom time!

SKIPPING SCHOOL

While an occasional day off should be allowed, truancy—cutting school—is a serious problem that can impact not only your child's education, but also his life.

If you discover that your child is cutting school, your first question should be: Why?

◆ Was he responding to peer pressure? Did his friends encourage him or dare him to do it? Have you been concerned about these kids for some time?

◆ Is something going on at school that he wants to avoid?

◆ Is this behavior out of sync with his usual personality?

◆ Are there familial issues impacting his behavior?

◆ Is he having academic problems? Is this something new? Are his problems concentrated in one class, or are they across the board?

The first time your student cuts school, you must respond with thoughtful, but deliberate action. You need to know *why* he chose this dangerous course before you can decide how to respond.

ALL IN THE FAMILY

 "Truancy is a stepping stone to delinquent and criminal activity. A report compiled by the Los Angeles County Office of Education on factors contributing to juvenile delinquency concluded that chronic absenteeism is the most powerful predictor of delinquent behavior... Truant students are at higher risk of being drawn into behavior involving drugs, alcohol, or violence."

Reprinted with permission from the pamphlet, "Truancy: First Step to a Lifetime of Problems," a publication of the Office of Juvenile Justice and Delinquency Prevention of the Department of Justice.

Attended	Milestone Moments (What did I learn or accomplish this week?)
☐	
☐	
☐	
☐	
☐	
☐	
☐	
☐	
☐	
☐	
☐	
☐	
☐	
☐	
☐	
☐	
☐	
☐	
☐	
☐	

The Little Gym® soar

Dance

Winter/Spring 2009 Themes

Getting Back on Track: Keep Your Cool

If you find out that your child is cutting school, you may be very angry, disappointed, and worried about him, but now's the time to keep your cool.

Your child may lose his temper, try to convince you that "Everyone does it," or promise fervently that he'll never cut school again. But the conversation isn't over. Only when you know *why* your child cut class can you decide what punishment is appropriate (if any).

Knowing *why* your student cut school will help you decide on an appropriate response. Here are some approaches to the problem:

◆ If you suspect that skipping school was indeed aberrant behavior for your child, a "once in a lifetime" incident, then grounding him or taking away social or phone privileges may be enough. But be sure that there isn't some underlying problem or that he isn't easily susceptible to peer pressure.

◆ If it's a problem with peer pressure, then you must work with your child to bolster his self-esteem and teach him problem-solving skills. He needs the self-confidence to choose the course of action that's right for him, no matter what his friends do.

Peer pressure is troubling since your child may also succumb to pressures about sex, drugs, and alcohol. If you're unhappy about his choice of friends, look for ways to introduce him to kids who share your values (see Chapter 1).

◆ If you believe that cutting class is symptomatic of a larger problem, make an appointment with the school counselor to discuss what's going on at school. Previously undiagnosed learning disabilities or a bad social situation may be affecting your child's education and making school a place he wants to avoid.

◆ You may also want to seek outside help if family pressures are taking a toll on your child. Cutting school may be a cry for help.

No matter what his explanation may be, you need to make clear that cutting school *isn't* the solution to his problems.

HELPING THE GIFTED AND TALENTED STUDENT

School should be a snap for kids who are exceptionally bright, but often that's not the case. Unless a bright child is engaged in active learning, she, too, can be turned off to school.

How can you tell if your child is gifted? Being gifted means more than being able to read at the age of two. Here are some indicators, reprinted from the ERIC Clearinghouse on Handicapped and Gifted Children (Reston, VA):

1. *General intellectual ability or talent.* Laypersons and educators alike usually define this in terms of a high intelligence score—usually two standard deviations above the mean—on individual or group measures. Parents and teachers often recognize students with general intellectual talent by their wide-ranging fund of general information and high levels of vocabulary, memory, abstract word knowledge, and abstract reasoning.

ALL IN THE FAMILY

Some sources cite IQ scores as a measure of intelligence. Scores are sometimes graded as follows:

- ◆ 85–99 Lower normal
- ◆ 100–114 Upper normal
- ◆ 115–129 Bright
- ◆ 130–144 Gifted
- ◆ 145–159 Highly gifted
- ◆ 160–above Profoundly gifted

---

2. *Specific academic aptitude or talent.* Students with specific academic aptitudes are identified by their outstanding performance on an achievement or aptitude test in one area (such as mathematics or language arts).

3. *Creative and productive thinking.* This is the ability to produce new ideas by bringing together elements usually thought of as independent or dissimilar and the aptitude for developing new

meanings that have social value. Characteristics of creative and productive students include openness to experience, setting personal standards for evaluation, ability to play with ideas, willingness to take risks, preference for complexity, tolerance for ambiguity, positive self-image, and the ability to become submerged in a task.

4. *Leadership ability.* Leadership can be defined as the ability to direct individuals or groups to a common decision or action. Students who demonstrate giftedness in leadership ability use group skills and negotiate in difficult situations. Many teachers recognize leadership through a student's keen interest and skill in problem solving. Leadership characteristics include self-confidence, responsibility, cooperation, a tendency to dominate, and the ability to adapt readily to new situations.

5. *Visual and performing arts.* Gifted students with talent in the arts demonstrate special talents in visual art, music, dance, drama, or other related studies.

Kids exhibit gifted behavior in many ways, although no child is outstanding in all characteristics. Here are some common signs of gifted behavior, reprinted from the ERIC Clearinghouse on Handicapped and Gifted Children (Reston, VA):

♦ Shows superior reasoning powers and marked ability to handle ideas; can generalize readily from specific facts and can see subtle relationships; has outstanding problem-solving ability.

♦ Shows persistent intellectual curiosity; asks searching questions; shows exceptional interest in the nature of man and the universe.

♦ Has a wide range of interests, often of an intellectual kind; develops one or more interests to considerable depth.

♦ Is markedly superior in quality and quantity of written and/or spoken vocabulary; is interested in the subtleties of words and their uses.

♦ Reads avidly and absorbs books well beyond his or her years.

♦ Learns quickly and easily and retains what is learned; recalls important details, concepts and principles; comprehends readily.

◆ Shows insight into arithmetical problems that require careful reasoning and grasps mathematical concepts readily.

◆ Shows creative ability or imaginative expression in such things as music, art, dance, drama; shows sensitivity and finesse in rhythm, movement, and bodily control.

◆ Sustains concentration for lengthy periods and shows outstanding responsibility and independence in classroom work.

◆ Sets realistically high standards for self; is self-critical in evaluating and correcting his or her own efforts.

◆ Shows initiative and originality in intellectual work; shows flexibility in thinking and considers problems from a number of viewpoints.

◆ Observes keenly and is responsive to new ideas.

◆ Shows social poise and an ability to communicate with adults in a mature way.

◆ Gets excitement and pleasure from intellectual challenge; shows an alert and subtle sense of humor.

MOM ALWAYS SAID

You may find that a highly gifted child is exceptional in some areas, but average or even below average in others. For example, she may have terrible handwriting because she thinks faster than she can write (or because her small motor control is not well developed). Or her spelling may be poor because she reads for comprehension and doesn't see words as collections of letters.

Gifted Children: A Mixed Blessing

Researchers often describe gifted children as "multiple-aged." That's because an exceptionally bright fourth grader may be reading on a twelfth-grade level and doing math on a ninth-grade level, but exhibiting the emotions of a second grader.

It's important for parents not to confuse their child's intellectual abilities with his age-appropriate behavior. It's important to remember he's still a kid. Your goal as the parent of a highly gifted child is to make sure that he's comfortable with his gifts and himself—and able to use his gifts productively.

Peer relationships are often hard for exceptionally bright kids. Often they feel isolated from other children because their interests and abilities are so very different. Here's how to help:

◆ Encourage your child to have different kinds of friends. There may be those his own age who he joins to play sports, watch TV, or shop. But he may also have older friends who meet his intellectual needs. (However, it's important for you to supervise his friendships with adults or older teens, since his judgment may still be at a disadvantage.)

◆ Consider enrolling your child in special programs for highly gifted children. Many colleges now sponsor summer classes for children who qualify. This gives the highly gifted student an opportunity to be with his peers.

◆ When your child becomes aware of his intellectual strengths, to help him keep things in perspective, remind him that his unusual intellectual ability, like his eye and hair color, is something he was born with. What's important is how he uses his gifts.

MOM ALWAYS SAID

Unlike children and adults with disabilities, gifted elementary and secondary school children have limited protection under state and federal laws to ensure that their education meets their needs. There is no legal requirement that a school district provide special programs for gifted students.

Gifted Kids at Home

You can best support your gifted child by respecting her needs—both intellectual and emotional. Like all kids, the very bright child needs limits, rules, guidelines, and positive feedback. It's easy to be swayed by her intellectual maturity, but it's important to remember: You're the mom. You're in charge.

Provide your child with the opportunity to serve others. Volunteer work is especially important for the highly gifted. It gives them a chance to learn tolerance, empathy, and an understanding of human limitations and the gifts inherent in all individuals.

Finally, make time for fun. Reserve time for family activities.

Gifted Kids in the Classroom

Obviously it's wonderful if your child is very bright, but it also raises a host of issues when you try to make sure that he receives a quality education. Highly gifted children not only learn faster than their peers, but also often learn differently.

The average child needs to have a complex subject divided into smaller, more manageable parts and presented one at a time, with frequent review. The highly gifted child thrives on complexity and can absorb material as a whole, with little repetition. It takes a talented teacher to make sure that the needs of all the children in the room are met.

In dealing with school issues, you need to trust your judgment about what's right for your child. Ideally, you should arrange a collaborative effort with your child's teacher and the school administration when working out a program in your child's best interests. Some school systems offer programs or magnet schools for gifted and talented children. Check with your principal for the criteria for selection. Other options include:

◆ *Acceleration.* Having your child skip grades (or enter school early) is a simple and economic approach to the problem of finding challenging material. But while your child's intellectual ability may be compatible with older kids, his social life may be seriously compromised. Researchers advise that it's best to accelerate girls before third grade or after ninth grade (when they are less connected to their peer group). Boys have less trouble skipping grades at any point in their academic program. A child's personal willingness to accelerate will help make the transition easier.

◆ *Subject matter acceleration.* You may choose to accelerate your child in only certain classes. For example, a highly gifted fifth grader may take math classes with eighth graders, English with seventh graders, and physical education with his own classmates. This can be a problem if a student must travel to different schools to take classes. Furthermore, when a child accelerates in a subject, by high school she may have taken all the classes available in that subject.

◆ *Home schooling.* Home schooling can be ideal for highly gifted children, meeting their intellectual needs and reinforcing their self-esteem. However, it can also strain familial relationships. Many kids need to keep the role of parent and the role of teacher separate. Parents who choose home schooling must also be sure that their children have frequent opportunities for social interaction with their peers. If you're interested in home schooling, check with your school district to see if it's legal and what requirements must be met.

MOM KNOWS BEST

If defined broadly, 10 to 15 percent of the students in any school system can be called gifted and talented.

MOM ALERT: ACADEMIC BURNOUT

Like adults, kids can also suffer from burnout: the feeling that it's all just *too* much (and, in fact, it often is). In our zeal to give our kids the opportunity to stretch and grow, they are sometimes overwhelmed by our demands and expectations or by their own expectations.

One third-grade teacher carefully explained to a gifted student that she was just trying to "stretch him" by giving him a difficult assignment. The child thoughtfully replied, "But suppose I break?" You want to walk a fine line between "stretching" your kids, but making sure they don't break.

All kids, and especially gifted ones, may get stressed when the going gets tough. The early grades may be easy for a gifted student, but as the work becomes more difficult, she may wonder how come she's not so smart anymore. Her self-esteem can be seriously compromised when the academic challenges seem daunting.

Furthermore, even with your best efforts to make your children understand that you love them for themselves, your kids may put incredible pressure on themselves to excel. Their own expectations may be far more demanding than any parental ones. The stress can take its toll. Here are some symptoms of burnout, reprinted with permission from the ERIC Clearinghouse on Handicapped and Gifted Children:

♦ Student is no longer happy or pleasantly excited about school activities, but, rather, is negative or cynical toward work, teachers, classmates, parents, and the whole school and achievement-centered experience.

♦ Student approaches most school assignments with resignation or resentment.

♦ Student exhibits boredom.

♦ Student suffers from sleeplessness, problems in falling asleep, or periodic waking.

♦ Student overreacts to normal concerns or events.

♦ Student exhibits unhappiness with self and accomplishments.

♦ Student has nervous habits such as rapid eye blinking, head shaking, or stuttering.

♦ Student has physical ailments such as weekly or daily stomachaches or headaches.

♦ Student is frequently ill.

♦ Student exhibits dependency through increased clinging or needing and demanding constant support and reassurance.

♦ Student engages in attention-getting behaviors such as aggressive or acting-out behaviors.

♦ Student has a sense of being trapped or a feeling of being out of control.

◆ Student is unable to make decisions.

◆ Student has lost perspective and sense of humor.

◆ Student experiences increased feelings of physical, emotional, and mental exhaustion in work and activities that used to give pleasure.

De-Stressing Your Student

If your child seems overburdened and stressed out, here's how you can help:

1. Talk about what's bothering him. Don't take "It's nothing" for an answer. If he's having problems with a specific class, make an appointment with the teacher. If more than one subject is troubling him, ask for a conference with all the teachers and the principal to get a "global" perspective on what's going on in school.

2. Listen carefully and sympathetically. Sometimes kids don't want a solution to their problems; they just want someone to listen nonjudgmentally.

3. Help your student learn organizational and time-management skills (see Chapter 3).

4. Insist he take regular physical exercise. He needs to channel some of his energy productively.

NOT LIVING UP TO POTENTIAL

It's so frustrating when you believe your child is not living up to her potential. Her grades may be C's when you know she's capable of getting B's, if not A's. Or she may get good grades, but refuse to challenge herself or to voluntarily work harder.

It's dangerous to label a child an "underachiever" because that term is an indictment of the child and ignores her positive achievements. The child who generally does poorly in school may excel in one specific subject, or may be outstanding in sports, social situations, or an outside job. *Focus on the specific behavior or situation you believe is troubling.* For example, you might describe your student as "underachieving" in math.

Underachievement becomes a self-fulfilling prophecy. Children who consider themselves underachievers may begin to see any academic success as a fluke and may refuse to even try to succeed at academic endeavors. But this negative self-concept can be overcome. Parents and teachers need to develop strategies that will reinforce a child's idea of herself as a learner:

♦ In the classroom, teachers should emphasize attempts, not just success; value student input in creating class rules and responsibilities; and encourage students to evaluate their own work before receiving a grade.

♦ Remedial work gives students opportunities to excel in an environment where mistakes are considered part of learning.

♦ Parents and teachers should recognize and encourage students whose performance or attitude begins to shift from "I can't" to "I most certainly can!"

Remember the goal is to encourage your student's own interest in learning. When he is self-motivated about his education, underachievement won't be an issue.

THE LEAST YOU NEED TO KNOW

♦ Many students declare at some point that they hate school. If your child displays a bad attitude toward school, find out if this is a temporary phase or a sign of a more significant problem.

♦ Truancy is a serious problem. If you discover that your child is skipping school, find out what's going on. Make sure your child is not being unduly influenced by peers or having serious academic difficulties.

♦ If your child is gifted, make sure her school is meeting her intellectual needs. Otherwise, she can be turned off to school.

♦ Labeling a child as an "underachiever" ignores her positive achievements. Instead, consider underachievement in context (for example, "underachieving in math"). Help your child develop a positive self-image as a learner.

13

We've Got a Problem

Of course you want your child to succeed in school, but sometimes problems develop that inhibit learning. If you suspect that your child has a learning disability that's affecting his ability to process information, early diagnosis and intervention is essential. Your child can, with professional help, master strategies for coping with and learning in spite of the disabilities. Whether the problem is temporary or long term, don't procrastinate (even if your student does) in seeking help.

HELP WANTED: FINDING THE RIGHT TUTOR

At some point in your student's academic career, she may need more assistance than you can provide. Or you may find that serving as your child's tutor is a constant source of irritation for the two of you, and that you need to step back and allow someone else to offer academic support.

Begin with your child's teacher, who should be able to provide additional help before, after, or during the school day. Even if your student has to get extra help on a daily basis, it may be enough to help her succeed in the class.

Your child shouldn't be embarrassed to ask for help; that is the teacher's job. Furthermore, many teachers prefer to assist students; some are uncomfortable with using outside tutors because the tutors may teach your child different techniques than the ones used in class.

If you find that your child is still having difficulty even though she's getting extra help from a teacher—or if you think the teacher may be part of the problem—then you will want to consider getting outside help.

Choosing the right tutor for your child isn't just a matter of finding someone knowledgeable in the subject. A good tutor not only knows his "stuff," but is also able to communicate effectively with your child.

But a good tutor needn't have a degree in education—or, for that matter, even be a college graduate. Some of the most effective tutors are peers. In some schools, honor society members offer a tutoring service; other districts maintain a list of student volunteer tutors. Other possible sources of tutors include retired teachers in the community (check the local senior center) and local college students (call the college student employment office).

Obviously, you'll pay more for an experienced adult tutor than you'll pay for a high school or college student. What you're looking for is someone who knows the subject and can effectively communicate it. Expect to pay between $6 to $10 per hour for a high school student and as much as $50 per hour for a retired teacher.

Before hiring a tutor:

♦ Review with him the material and text you expect him to cover.

♦ Check his references. Ask specifically about his ability to teach; he may know his subject very well, but can he effectively communicate that knowledge?

♦ Work out the logistics of where and when the tutoring sessions will be held. Continuity is important, so establish a schedule of tutoring sessions.

CHEATING: A CAUSE FOR CONCERN

Honesty and integrity are core values that parents try to instill in their children. So the accusation that your child has cheated can be a devastating blow. But this is the time to keep your cool and use all your parenting skills to help your student rediscover her fundamental values.

The first question is *why.* Talk to your child. Did she feel pressure to produce good grades—at any cost? Was it peer pressure? Was she trying to please you? Does she have unreasonable expectations of herself? Is the class too difficult?

Make an appointment to talk to the teacher and school administrators. You need to know if this was a one-time event or a recurring behavior. You also want to know what action the school is taking. Although there should be consequences for your child's conduct, punishment isn't really the point. You want your child to understand that cheating is unacceptable, not because the consequences are dire, but because it's fundamentally dishonest to everyone, herself most of all.

Then you and your child need to come up with a solution to the underlying problem. It's time for a serious conversation with your child. Here's what you should discuss and do:

◆ *Make sure your student understands that your love is unconditional.* Grades in academic subjects don't influence how you feel about her and shouldn't affect how she feels about herself. Remind her that it's the learning that's important, not the grade.

◆ *Remind your student that asking for help is a sign of maturity.* If your child feels she's in over her head with her classwork, get her help. That may mean withdrawing from the particular class or getting a tutor.

◆ *Help your student get organized.* Time management skills will help your child use her study time more effectively. (See Chapters 2, 3, and 4.)

◆ *Model the honest behavior you want your student to live.* Make sure your child sees that you lead the kind of honest life that you want her to live. Did the cashier at the supermarket give you a quarter extra? Give it back (even if it means returning from the parking lot). That moment of honesty will give your child a lifelong message.

LEARNING DISABLED—BUT LEARNING

The term *learning disabled* (LD) sounds ominous, but many successful adults have learned to compensate for their disabilities. George Bush, for example, is dyslexic. It's estimated that 15 to 20 percent of the U.S. population has some learning disability. Learning disabilities often run in families.

WISE WORDS

Learning disabilities are defined as lifelong, neurologically based conditions that interfere with one's ability to store, process, and retrieve information.

Learning disabilities can affect reading, writing, speaking, and mathematical abilities, and they can inhibit social skills. Learning disabilities create a wide gap between potential and performance, but LD children and adults are of average or above-average intelligence.

ALL IN THE FAMILY

Early intervention and diagnosis of learning disabilities is critical.

◆ 50 percent of juvenile delinquents tested were found to have previously undetected learning disabilities.

◆ 35 percent of LD students drop out of high school.

◆ 17 to 60 percent of teens in treatment for drug and alcohol abuse have learning disabilities.

Is My Child LD?

The National Center for Learning Disabilities has developed a guidepost of common warning signs of LD. But remember: All kids exhibit one or more of these behaviors from time to time. A *consistent* display of a *group* of these behaviors should be considered an indication to seek further advice.

Common Warning Signs—A Checklist

DOES THE INDIVIDUAL HAVE DIFFICULTY WITH:

Organization

Knowing time, date, year	Carrying out a plan
Managing time	Making decisions
Completing assignments	Setting priorities
Organizing thoughts	Sequencing
Locating belongings	

Physical Coordination

Manipulating small objects	Handwriting
Learning self-help skills	Climbing and running
Cutting	Mastering sports
Drawing	

Spoken or Written Language

Pronouncing words	Responding to questions
Learning new vocabulary	Understanding concepts
Following directions	Reading comprehension
Understanding requests	Spelling
Relating stories	Writing stories and essays
Discriminating among sounds	

Attention and Concentration

Completing a task	Restlessness
Acting before thinking	Daydreaming
Poor organization	Distractibility
Waiting	

Common Warning Signs—A Checklist (*continued*)

DOES THE INDIVIDUAL HAVE DIFFICULTY WITH:

Memory

Remembering directions	Remembering names
Learning math facts	Remembering events
Learning new procedures	Spelling
Learning the alphabet	Studying for tests
Identifying letters	

Social Behavior

Making and keeping friends	Sportsmanship
Social judgment	Accepting changes in routine
Impulsive behavior	Interpreting nonverbal cues
Frustration tolerance	Working cooperatively

From the National Center for Learning Disabilities, 381 Park Avenue South, Suite 1401, New York, NY 10016; phone 1-888-575-7373.

First Signs of Trouble

Although many children have difficulty from time to time with one or more of the items listed below, if you suspect your child has a learning disability, you have to consider her problem areas in the context of her overall abilities and development. If you're concerned, seek further assessment. Talk to your family pediatrician, your child's classroom teacher, and the school guidance counselor.

What to Look for: Some First Signs of Trouble

SKILL	PROBLEM
	Lower Grades
Language	Delayed decoding abilities for reading.
	Trouble following directions.
	Poor spelling.
Memory	Slow recall of facts.
	Organizational problems.
	Slow acquisition of new skills.
	Poor spelling.

Attention	Impulsivity, lack of planning.
	Careless errors.
	Insatiability.
	Distractibility.
Fine-motor skills	Unstable pencil grip.
	Trouble with letter formation.
Other functions	Trouble learning about time (temporal-sequential disorganization).
	Poor grasp of math concepts.

Middle Grades

Language	Poor reading comprehension.
	Lack of verbal participation in class.
	Trouble with word problems.
Memory	Poor or illegible writing.
	Slow or poor recall of math facts.
	Failure of automatic recall.
Attention	Inconsistency.
	Poor self-monitoring.
	Great knowledge of trivia.
	Distaste for fine detail.
Fine-motor skills	Fist-like or tight pencil.
	Illegible, slow, or inconsistent writing.
	Reluctance to write.
Other functions	Poor learning strategies.
	Disorganization in time or space.
	Peer rejection.

Upper Grades

Language	Weak grasp of explanations.
	Foreign language problems.
	Poor written expression.
	Trouble summarizing.
Memory	Trouble studying for tests.
	Weak cumulative memory.
	Slow work pace.

What to Look for: Some First Signs of Trouble (*continued*)

SKILL	PROBLEM
Attention	Memory problems due to weak attention.
	Mental fatigue.
Fine-motor skills	Lessening relevance of fine-motor skills.
Other functions	Poor grasp of abstract concepts.
	Failure to elaborate.
	Trouble taking multiple-choice tests, (for example, SAT's).

Melvin D. Levine, M.D., F.A.A.P., THEIR WORLD, 1990.

From the National Center for Learning Disabilities, 381 Park Avenue South, Suite 1401, New York, NY 10016; phone 1-888-575-7373.

Common Learning Disabilities

There are many types of learning disabilities; only a professional can evaluate and diagnose whether your child is LD and to what extent. Here are some of the more common learning disabilities:

◆ *Apraxia (Dyspraxia)* The inability to motor plan, to make an appropriate body response.

◆ *Dysgraphia* Difficulty with the act of writing, both in the technical as well as the expressive sense. Also difficulty with spelling.

◆ *Dyssemia* Difficulty with signals (i.e., social cues).

◆ *Auditory Discrimination* Difficulty perceiving the differences between sounds and the sequences of sounds.

◆ *Visual Perception* Difficulty understanding what one sees.

From the National Center for Learning Disabilities, 381 Park Avenue South, Suite 1401, New York, NY 10016; phone 1-888-575-7373.

If You Suspect a Problem

If you suspect that your child has a learning disability, you must get accurate information. Your own instincts may be correct, but your child must be evaluated by a team of professionals who will use a variety of standardized tests and informal tasks to reach a diagnosis. The team may include a pediatrician, a pediatric neurologist, a psychologist, an occupational therapist, and a classroom and learning disabilities teacher.

Under the law, you can request an evaluation if you suspect your child has a learning disability. Talk to the school counselor or school psychologist.

MOM KNOWS BEST

The Individuals with Disabilities Education Act requires public school systems to evaluate referred students to determine if special education services are warranted. Referrals can be made by parents or professionals, but evaluation requires parental consent.

If you choose to have your child privately evaluated, check with your school system. Some districts don't honor test results from sources outside the school system.

Other parents of LD children can be a wonderful source of information and support. Keep in mind, however, that what works for one child or family may not be applicable to your child's circumstances. You'll need to tailor the resources in your school system and community to your own child's needs.

If your child has a learning disability, you'll have to be your child's advocate:

◆ You're entitled to have a say in the educational decisions that affect your child.

◆ You should learn how to request services for your student, including evaluation and treatment.

◆ You should make sure to understand the proposed treatment plan and monitor its implementation and effectiveness.

◆ You may have to serve as the facilitator and coordinator of the personnel assigned to your child's case. There may be several members of your student's remediation team, and you may be the only one to see the whole picture, not just the individual components.

Supporting an LD Child

If your child is diagnosed with a learning disability, here are the two most important ways you can help:

◆ Never humiliate or embarrass your child. An LD child's self-esteem is especially fragile.

◆ No matter what learning disabilities your student may have, remember she is, above all else, still a child. Even with additional time needed for studying and remediation, it's important to plan time for fun. Let your student be a kid.

ATTENTION DEFICIT (HYPERACTIVITY) DISORDER

Reports about the growing number of children diagnosed with *Attention Deficit (Hyperactivity) Disorder (ADD or ADHD)* have made many parents and educators wary. Do all kids who can't seem to sit still suffer from ADHD? Are we overmedicating young children with Ritalin and other similar medications? Or are we finally addressing a real problem that can seriously affect a child's ability to learn?

ADHD is a neurologically based disorder. It has three main symptoms: distractibility, impulsivity, and hyperactivity. But these same symptoms can be evidence of anxiety and/or depression. Children with ADD share the symptoms of distractibility and impulsivity, but not hyperactivity. The dominant symptom of ADD is *hypo-activity* (daydreaming or tuning out). ADD and ADHD are not learning disabilities, but many children who suffer from these disorders also have learning disabilities. That's why any diagnosis of ADD/ADHD should include a comprehensive educational assessment.

Children who suffer from these disorders may have difficulty socially. They are prone to angry outbursts and self-imposed social isolation. They are often quick to fight and to blame others for their problems. Furthermore, they show a high sensitivity to criticism. This can make it difficult to live with an ADHD/ADD child—and this is why it's especially important to get an accurate diagnosis and begin treatment. Parents with an ADHD/ADD child will benefit from being in a support group with other parents who live with the same pressures.

Is Medication the Answer?

Ritalin (or similar medications) has been used for 30 years in the treatment of Attention Deficit (Hyperactivity) Disorder. It's been very effective, and its side effects are well known. However, only a doctor should decide if Ritalin is appropriate treatment. Although the doctor may ask for a teacher's observations, educators are not qualified to make an assessment about the medication's use.

Whether your doctor prescribes medication or other nonmedical therapies, careful monitoring is essential.

DEALING WITH FAILURE

Failing grades can deal a blow not just to a child's academic average, but to her ego as well. Make sure that the failure is kept in perspective. Here's what you should do if your child brings home a failing grade:

1. Remind your student that your love is not dependent on her grades.

2. If the failing grade is a surprise, then you need to figure out why you didn't know that your student was struggling.

3. Remind your student that the point of education is to learn the material, not the score on a report card.

Once you've taken these steps, it's time to figure out what to do to salvage a difficult situation.

Ask your student what she thinks is going on. Did she fail an individual test, an entire course, or is there a downward spiral to all her grades? If it's an isolated test grade, then work with her to improve her study habits to meet the demands of the course. If your child believes that the material is too difficult, find out what kind of additional help she has been getting (if any). Do you suspect learning disabilities?

Determine what else is going on in her life. Is she too involved in extra-curricular activities? Is her social life affecting her academics?

If you believe that she's spending too much time on the phone or with friends, and too little on studies, then work out a reasonable schedule that balances her schoolwork and social life. Don't ground her completely or turn off the phone. You want to avoid isolating your child or creating such an atmosphere of antagonism that school becomes a source of conflict. Instead, help your child realize that she needs to develop a balance in her life.

Next, you want to provide your student with support both on the home front and in school. Make an appointment with her teacher and, if necessary, her guidance counselor. See if the teacher's assessment of the situation jibes with your child's. Talk about what steps can be taken to be sure that your student passes the course.

If passing the course is no longer possible, find out what's next. Does she need the course in order to graduate? If so, should she repeat the class the following year or can she enroll in summer school? Will the failing grade remain on her transcript? Will the summer school grade also appear? Can a letter of explanation be added to her file?

ALL IN THE FAMILY

Between 5 and 7 percent of public school children repeat a grade each year. By ninth grade, about 50 percent of students have failed at least one grade or have dropped out. But studies show that when retained students finally go on to the next grade, they actually perform more poorly on average than if they had gone on without repeating.

Alternatives to Retention

Grade retention, studies show, is not generally effective in ensuring basic skills mastery, nor does repeating a grade necessarily avoid failure at higher grade levels or lower dropout rates. Retained students also tend to have more problems with social adjustment, a negative attitude toward school, behavior problems, and are more likely to be truant. Students who repeat a grade are also at higher risk of dropping out. *Grade retention should be the last resort.*

Alternatives that have proven more effective include: remedial help; before and after-school programs; summer school; peer tutoring; and having instructional classroom aides work with high-risk students.

THE LEAST YOU NEED TO KNOW

- ◆ If your student is having academic problems, get help early. Peer tutors, college students, and retired teachers are often available for tutoring.

- ◆ If your child is caught cheating, find out why she cheated. Make sure she understands that the point of education is learning new material, not scoring a particular grade.

- ◆ Early diagnosis and intervention can teach students strategies for coping with learning disabilities.

- ◆ If your student is failing a test, a course, or several subjects, it's vitally important that you reassure him that your love is unconditional. Then you can determine what's causing the problem and how to solve it.

- ◆ Grade retention can be severely detrimental to a student's self-esteem and attitude toward school.

Resources

SUGGESTED READING LIST

Berge, Margaret and Philip Gibbons. *Help Your Child Excel in Math.* Hollywood: Lifetime Books, 1992.

Boegehold, Betty D. *Getting Ready to Read.* New York: Ballantine Books, 1984.

Brown, Martha C. and Jeremy P. Tarcher. *Schoolwise.* Los Angeles: 1985.

Cullinan, Bernice E. *Read to Me.* New York: Scholastic, Inc., 1992.

Cutright, Melitta J. *The National PTA Talks to Parents.* New York: Doubleday, 1989.

Dunn, Rita, Kenneth Dunn, and Donald Treffinger. *Bringing Out the Giftedness in Your Child.* New York: John Wiley & Sons, 1992.

Eisenberg, Ronni with Kate Kelly. *Organize Your Family.* New York: Hyperion, 1993.

Frith, Terry. *Secrets Parents Should Know About Public Schools.* New York: Simon and Schuster, 1985.

Graves, Donald and Virginia Stuart. *Write From The Start.* New York: E.P. Dutton, 1985.

Keogh, James. *Getting the Best Education for Your Child.* Los Angeles: Lowell House, 1996.

Lee, Barbara and Masha Kabakow Rudman. *Mind Over Media.* New York: Seaview Books, 1982.

McInally, Pat. *Moms & Dads Kids & Sports.* New York: Charles Scribner's Sons, 1988.

Pipher, Mary. *Reviving Ophelia.* New York: G.P. Putnam's Sons, 1994.

Radencich, Marguerite C. and Jeanne Shay Schumm. *How to Help Your Child With Homework.* Minneapolis: Free Spirit Publishing, 1988.

Silberman, Arlene. *Growing Up Writing.* New York: Times Books, 1989.

Trelease, Jim. *The Read-Aloud Handbook.* New York: Penguin Books, 1982.

Weiner, Harvey S. *Any Child Can Read Better.* New York: Oxford University Press, 1996.

Wiener, Harvey S. *Any Child Can Write.* New York: Oxford University Press, 1994.

Wolff, Rick. *Good Sports.* New York: Dell Publishing, 1993.

Yablum, Ronn. *How To Develop Your Child's Gifts and Talents in Math.* Los Angeles: Lowell House, 1995.

WEB SITES OF INTEREST

Parent Institute
http://www.par-inst.com

Internet Resources for Parents and Those Who Work with Parents
http://ericps.ed.uiuc.edu/npin/parlink.html

Superkids Educational Software Review: The Parents' and Teachers' Guide to Children's Software
http://www.superkids.com/aweb/pages/contents.html

Family Pages
Links to Web sites of interest
http://www.nauticom.net/www/cokids/Familyl.html

Moms Online
Cybercommunity with bulletin boards, chat rooms, and resources
MomsOnline@aol.com

ParentSoup
Cybercommunity with bulletin boards, chat rooms, and resources
ParentSoup@aol.com

Parents Place
Cybercommunity with bulletin boards, chat rooms, and resources
http://www.parentsplace.com

Favorite Education Places on Web
Links to resources
http://www.clp.berkeley.edu/CLP/education.html

Study Skills Self Help Information
http://www.vt.edu:10021/studentinfo/ucc/stdyhlp.html

Links to Educational Resources
http://www.yahoo.com/Education/K-12/Resources/

Cool School Tools
Index to Internet and World Wide Web resources
http://www.bham.lib.al.us/cooltools/

Software and Web Pages for Girls
http://www.interactive.net/~shannah/girls/software.html

National PTA
http://www.pta.org

RESOURCES

The following organizations are good sources of information, publications, referrals, and support. The accompanying reading lists offer additional insight and tips.

Reading

International Reading Association

A nonprofit education organization devoted to the improvement of reading instruction and the promotion of the lifelong reading habit.

Parent Booklets are available for $2 each, prepaid. Send check to Parent Booklets at the International Reading Association, 800 Barksdale Road, P.O. Box 8139, Newark, DE 19714-8139. Specify both title and publication number when ordering.

◆ *Beginning Literacy and Your Child.* Steven B. Silvern and Linda R. Silvern. No. 164.

◆ *Creating Readers and Writers.* Susan Mandel Glazer. No. 165.

◆ *Encouraging Your Junior High Student to Read.* John Shefelbine. No. 168.

◆ *Helping Your Child Become a Reader.* Nancy L. Roser. No. 161.

◆ *How Can I Prepare My Young Child for Reading?* Paula C. Grinnell. No. 163.

- *You Can Encourage Your High School Student to Read.* Jamie Myers. No. 162.

- *You Can Help Your Young Child with Writing.* Marcia Baghban. No. 160.

- *Your Child's Vision is Important.* Caroline Beverstock. No. 167.

Attention Deficit (Hyperactivity) Disorder (ADD & ADHD)

Attention Deficit Information Network, Inc.
475 Hillside Avenue
Needham, MA 02914
(617) 455-9895

Children and Adults with ADD (CHADD)
499 NW 70th Avenue, #308
Plantation, FL 33317
(954) 587-3700

Learning Disabilities

ERIC Clearinghouse on Disabilities and Gifted Education
1920 Association Drive
Reston, VA 22091-1589
(800) 328-0272

Learning Disabilities Association of America
4156 Library Road
Pittsburgh, PA 15234
(412) 341-1515

Orton Dyslexia Society
8600 La Salle Road, #382
Baltimore, MD 21286-2044
(410) 825-2881

Gifted and Talented Children

ERIC Clearinghouse on Disabilities and Gifted Education
1920 Association Drive
Reston, VA 22091-1589
(800) 328-0272

The Comprehensive Gifted Resources home page contains links to all known online gifted resources, enrichment programs, talent searches, and early acceptance programs: http://www.eskimo.com/~user/kids.html.

Index

A

academic burnout, 153-154
academic cheating, 159
academic stress, 155
accomplishments, recording in scrapbooks, 7
ACT (American College Test) testing, 47-48
all-girl math classes, 112
America Online, homework help, 32-33
apraxia, 164
Ask Dr. Math Web site, 109
assessing learning disabilities, 162-164
assigning household chores, 9
Attention Deficit Disorder (ADD),
    166-167, 174
auditory learners, 37-38

B

balancing
  core courses with elective courses, 126-127
  schoolwork versus job resposibilities, 140
band, joining, 136-137
believing in children, 6
board games and math activities, 107
books
  difficulty levels, 79
  for reluctant readers, 80-81
  geography-related, 123-124
  history-related, 121-123
  reading with aid of dictionary, 80
boys, reading preferences, 86
building self-esteem, 7
bulletin boards, 16

C

calculating grades, weighted factors, 66
cheating behavior, 159
child labor laws, 141
children
  academic burnout, 153-154
  academic stress, 155
  accomplishments, recording, 7
  addiction to praise, 7-8
  Attention Deficit Disorder (ADD), 174
  believing in, 6
  career days, 61
  cheating, 159

collecting activities, 137-138
  ground rules, 138
  Internet research, 138
constructive praise, 7-8
dislike for school, 144
educational goals, setting, 4
failing grades, 167-168
failures, dealing with, 8
gifted, 175
  academic versus emotional behavior,
    150-151
  at-home behavior, 151-152
  indicators, 148-150
homework difficulties, 30
household chores, assigning, 9
learning disabilites, 174
learning types, determining, 38-41
limits, establishing, 6
organized sports
  cut from team, 134
  quitting, 135
parent-teacher conferences, 57-58
peer influence, 2
permanent school records, 73
problem teachers, 50-53
questionable friends, handling, 3
reading and family story hour, 82
reluctant readers, 80-81
requesting new teacher, 54
requests for specific teachers, 55-56
schools
  absences, 145
  peer pressure, 147
  skipping, 146
schoolwork, minimum requirements, 9-10
self-esteem, building, 7
stress indicators, 10
teacher complaints, resolving, 53-54
television
  controlling, 11-12
  responsible viewing, 11
truancy problems, 147
tutors
  finding, 158
  hiring, 158
  hourly pay, 158
unconditional love, 6
underachievement, 155-156
volunteer work, 139
writing activities at home, 91-92

177

ABOUT THE AUTHORS

Vicki Poretta is the creator of the *Mom's Guide* publications. Vicki, who is active in her kids' interests in sports, came up with the idea for *Mom's Guide* publications while trying to answer many of her children's sports-related questions. After searching unsuccessfully for books that could offer concise information on the rules to different sports, she joined forces with Big World Media, Inc., of Boston, to produce and distribute a series of Game-time Reference Guides which explain the basic rules and terms to the sports that kids play.

Marian Edelman Borden has written several parent-friendly books on education, including *In Addition to Tuition, The Parents' Survival Guide to Freshman Year of College* and *Smart Start, The Parents' Complete Guide to Preschool Education* (both published by Facts on File). Her work has appeared in *American Baby, Parenting,* and the *New York Times.* She is the mother of four children, all good students, and one dog, an obedience school dropout.